Lipids
in
Human
Nutrition

Lipids in Human Nutrition

An Appraisal of Some Dietary Concepts

GERMAIN J. BRISSON, Ph.D.
Professor of Nutrition
Université Laval, Québec, Canada

Englewood, New Jersey

JACK K. BURGESS, INC.
1981

JACK K. BURGESS, INC.
44 Engle Street, Englewood, New Jersey 07631, USA

Library of Congress Cataloging in Publication Data

Brisson, Germain J.
   Lipids in human nutrition.

   Includes bibliographical references and index.
   1. Lipids in nutrition. 2. Lipids—
Metabolism. 3. Nutritionally induced diseases.

I. Title.

QP751.B73   612'.397   81-17013

ISBN 0-937218-12-X   AACR2

Library of Congress Catalog Card Number 81-17013
International Standard Book Number 0-937218-12-X

Printed in the United States of America

To my wife Yvette

and children

Jacques
Jean-Claude
Suzanne
Paul-André
Lise

Contents

Foreword

Throughout its history, medicine has benefited from scientific discoveries made in complementary fields such as chemistry, physics and biology. Thus, in the middle of the last century, the works of Pasteur, a chemist and biologist, by revealing the world of micro-organisms, bacteria and viruses, made it possible to control a considerable number of often fatal diseases.

Guided by the work of this inspired biologist, the English surgeon, Sir Joseph Lister, developed aseptic techniques which have rendered possible the spectacular achievements of modern surgery. It is largely due to such advances that the life-expectancy of man, 50 years at the turn of the century (1900), approaches 75 years in 1981.

Even today, however, in spite of this, two groups of ailments, arteriosclerosis and cancer, are responsible for 70 per cent of human deaths both in Canada and in the United States of America. The former is a degenerative process of the arterial system, the latter an uncontrolled and destructive cellular proliferation.

Although several predisposing factors are known, the essential cause of these conditions is wholly unknown. As long as this ignorance of the etiology persists, all forms of therapy can be no more than palliative.

Congenital impairment of lipid metabolism enables us to ascertain the disastrous effects of hypercholesterolemia in subjects aged from 20 to 40 who exhibit degeneration of the arterial walls normally seen in older people aged 70–80. But the significance of the cholesterol level in normal subjects, that is those who are not genetically deficient, is much less convincing.

The role of certain lipids, particularly cholesterol, long thought to be risk factors in sclerosis of the arteries, is today again an open question. In cancer, recent studies tend to establish a relationship between the ingestion of certain lipids and the frequency of malignant tumors of breast and intestine.

In trying to throw light on the enigma of the "trans" fatty acids, a by-product of the vegetable-oil industry, and in explaining the effects of blood cholesterol and lipoproteins in the development of cardiovascular disease, Professor Brisson acquaints us with some real problems of modern medicine.

In a clear style, and generously illustrated, the author familiarizes us with the language of science and with the role of different fats in nutrition. He shows their importance in the functioning of the different organs and tissues of the body.

Referring to the clinical trials of the last several years, based on the administration of hypolipemic agents and significant and prolonged changes in diet, the author ends by casting serious doubt on the hyperlipemic origin of cardiovascular disease in man. He makes an appeal for restraint in the use of partially hydrogenated vegetable oils because of their high content of "trans" fatty acids, the effects of which on vascular sclerosis and in tumor induction are a cause for concern.

Professor Germain Brisson's book is highly topical. It is informative, demystifying and reassuring. It marks the end of an era of futile dietary austerity which has now lasted more than twenty-five years, has been responsible for much writing and argument, has given rise to the most unusual diets, has led to almost dietary "religions" and above all, most unfortunately, has, for millions of individuals, seasoned each meal with a bitter taste of guilt. A careful reading of this book should facilitate a return to common sense in the field of nutrition.

For the well informed public, these chapters are a source of valuable information readily understood and of the nature to dispel certain collective phobias. For the therapist they offer an explanation which allows him to bring up-to-date earlier, sometimes tendentious, ideas on the role of lipids in both nutrition and human pathology.

Doctor, health-professional, scientist, educator, or simply a curious reader, we all have the opportunity to move with ease into the world of lipids. This book, by Doctor Germain Brisson, biochemist and nutrition-specialist, contains all that is needed to guide us.

Pierre R. Grondin, M.D., O.C.
Director, Cardiovascular Center,
St. Francis Hospital,
Miami Beach, Florida

Preface

The publication of this book may surprise some researchers in the fields of lipids and nutrition because much of its content has been available to them through the scientific literature. They are constantly working in these areas and their knowledge is always current. However, those in other fields, for example physicians, are less fortunate; they have to monitor knowledge in a broad spectrum of disciplines. Moreover, most of the research on lipids and nutrition is not only reported in highly specialized scientific literature, to which physicians, dietitians, nurses and other health professionals may not have easy access, but it is often couched in scientific jargon which is difficult to understand and quickly becomes disheartening. It is not surprising, therefore, that adjustments to accepted theories in any specialist field may take a long time—perhaps years—before they are generally recognized and accepted by those in other fields.

Lipids constitute a large proportion of the total calories in the North American diet. During the past three decades, the effects on health of both the amount and type of fat consumed have been the subject of numerous investigations. The purpose of this book is to present an analysis of the current knowledge of some of the roles of lipids in human nutrition and appraise some dietary aspects. An effort is made to use common language and to give an explanation for the principles involved. It is based on data published mostly during the past decade and offers a new look on a subject which is still a matter of some controversy.

The book is addressed primarily to physicians, but dietitians, nurses and other health professionals will find it of interest. Those in the field of food science and food production have a responsibility with regard to the quality and wholesomeness of our food supply; lipids represent an important part of this supply. Those in the field of animal science and animal production are concerned with the controversy surrounding animal fats. These professionals and students in all these fields of endeavor will find information here which is of interest to them. Finally, consumers with some training in human physiology will gain a better understanding of the role of dietary fat in their every day life.

Acknowledgements

The completion of this book would have been impossible without the help of many people. I am particularly grateful to Dr. Jack Cameron, Ph.D., Institut Armand-Frappier, Laval-des-Rapides, Quebec, who worked with me in developing the English manuscript from the translation made by Marcel Séguin. Drs. Jean-Claude Dillon, M.D., Ph.D., and Jacques Brisson, M.D., D.Sc., Université Laval, and Professor J. M. Bell, Ph.D., University of Saskatoon, made valuable comments and suggestions. The figures and tables were conceived and designed by Jean-Claude Brisson, P.Eng., M.Sc. They were revised and adapted by the artists of La boîte à graphe, Montreal. Suzanne Brisson and Christiane Morency assisted in preparing the documentation. Lise Brisson and Claudette Laurence patiently typed the different versions of the manuscript. Carole Noël and Gilles Goulet revised the french manuscript. The pertinent suggestions made by the Publisher, Jack K. Burgess, were greatly appreciated.

Finally, I wish to acknowledge the patience and sustained understanding of my wife during the many hours of study and work required for the preparation of this book.

Quebec, 1981   GERMAIN J. BRISSON

"Derrière ma médecine, ma nutrition, il y a le Vivant. Je suis dans la Science du Vivant. J'ai à l'enseigner, à l'appliquer. J'ai à la rendre utile dans la transformation du milieu de nos vies."

Jean Trémolières

(Textes posthumes)

1
Dietary fats and body lipids: terms used

INTRODUCTION

Fats have physical, chemical and physiological properties which make them important both in nutrition and in food technology. In addition to fats ingested as food, there are specific lipids synthesized by the human body which are essential to life. To understand best the role of fats in the diet, some basic information concerning the chemical nature of such important molecules and certain aspects of their metabolism is necessary. In this chapter, information will be given on the different molecules which are referred to throughout the book, and on their structure.

Properties of lipids

Lipids form a group of compounds the chemical nature of which is extremely varied. Yet they have the common property of being soluble in organic solvents such as benzene, ether, chloroform and mixtures of chloroform and methanol. They are insoluble in water and this basic property affects profoundly the particular phenomena associated with their digestion, absorption, transport in the blood and metabolism at the cellular level. The latter property also determines the particular processes used in food technology for their extraction, purification and transformation.

FATTY ACIDS

Fatty acids are the main constituents of food fats and oils as well as of depot fats in man and animals. They are composed solely of carbon, hydrogen and oxygen; on a weight basis, these three elements are found in the proportions of 76.0, 12.7 and 11.3 per cent respectively. The high proportion of carbon as compared to hydrogen and oxygen is to be noted. The fatty acid molecules consist of carbon atoms linked to one another to form a chain varying in length from 4 to 26 carbons. In general, the carbon chain of fatty acids in vegetable and animal fats has an even number of carbon atoms.

An example of a fatty acid molecule is given in Fig 1; it has a chain length of 18 carbon atoms. The length of the carbon chain is an important feature of fatty acids found in foods and in the human body.

Saturated, monounsaturated and polyunsaturated fatty acids

The methyl group at one end of the chain consists of three hydrogen atoms linked to the terminal carbon atom. However, the carbon atoms which form the body of the chain have only two positions where hydrogen atoms can be fixed, the other two being used to form the carbon–to–carbon bonds. If all the available positions are occupied by hydrogen atoms, the molecule becomes a saturated fatty acid (Fig 1). If, on the other hand, one hydrogen atom is missing from each of two neighbouring carbons, the free bonds form a second carbon–to–carbon link, a double bond, and the fatty acid is said to be monounsaturated. The fatty acid becomes polyunsaturated if two or more double bonds are formed on the carbon chain. An example of a polyunsaturated fatty acid is given in Fig 2.

Nomenclature

It is sometimes difficult to understand publications dealing with lipids because of the terminology used. The nomenclature of fatty acids is complex and although standardized it may still vary from one author to another. It is complex because only one term or symbol is used to indicate the many characteristics of these compounds: chain length, degree of saturation or unsaturation and position of the double bond or bonds on the chain. The different terms and symbols used to describe chemically the principal fatty acids found in foods of animal or vegetable origin are given in Table 1.

The nomenclature of saturated fatty acids does not present any difficulty as their main feature is simply chain length. For example, stearic acid, a saturated fatty acid with a chain length of 18 carbons (Fig 1), may easily be designated by the symbol C18:0. According to the systematic nomenclature this acid is called *n*-octadecanoic acid. The terms adopted in this form of nomenclature are gradually being introduced into the literature dealing with lipids, but they are not yet in general use.

The terminology of monounsaturated and polyunsaturated fatty acids presents more difficulties because, in addition to chain length, indications must be given as to the number of double carbon bonds and their respective positions on the chain. Double bonds are indicated by the symbols Δ, ω or *n* followed by one or more numbers giving their position on the carbon chain. In this case, carbon atoms may be numbered from the carboxyl (Δ nomenclature) or from the methyl (ω or *n* nomenclature) group. Taking

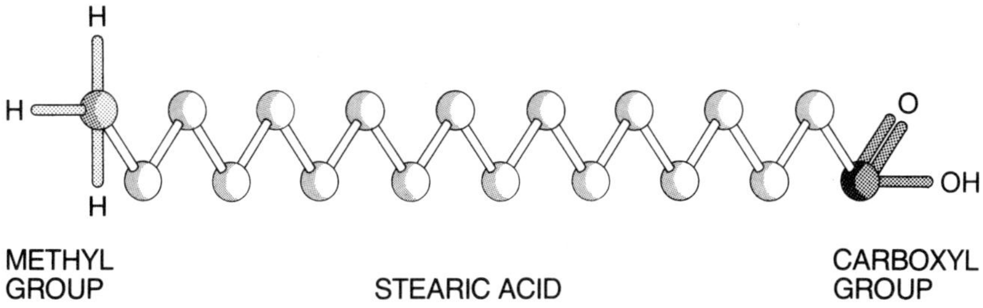

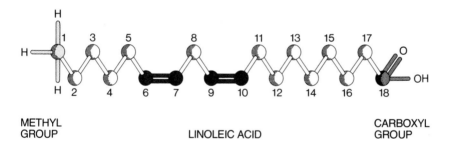

H

H

H

METHYL
GROUP   STEARIC ACID

O

OH

CARBOXYL
GROUP

Fig. 1—*Schematic illustration of a fatty acid with an* 18-*carbon
chain.*

Each carbon atom has four bonds. At one end of the chain, a
carbon atom is bound to three hydrogen atoms to form a methyl
group ($—CH_3$); at the other end the carbon is bound to an oxygen
atom (=O) and a hydroxyl group (—OH) to form a carboxyl group
(—COOH). In this case, all carbon atoms forming the body of the
chain are saturated with hydrogen atoms ($—CH_2—CH_2$ . . .).

METHYL
GROUP   LINOLEIC ACID

CARBOXYL
GROUP

Fig. 2—*Schematic illustration of a polyunsaturated fatty acid
molecule.*

Unsaturated fatty acids have one or more double bonds along the
carbon chain. At these points of unsaturation there is a loss of two
hydrogen atoms, one on each of the two carbons involved. Monounsaturated fatty acids have only one double bond while the
polyunsaturated ones have two or more. Carbon atoms are numbered from the terminal carboxyl or methyl group, depending on
the particular nomenclature being used. The symbol Δ preceeding
a number means that the carbon atoms are numbered from the
terminal carboxyl group whereas the symbols ω and *n* mean that
numbering is done from the terminal methyl group.

---

linoleic acid as an example (Fig 2), the symbol $\Delta^{9.12}$ indicates a carbon chain with two double bonds, the first one located on the 9th carbon counting from the carboxyl group and the second one on the 12th carbon. The formula C18:2ω6 could also designate linoleic acid, but the symbol ω6 then means that the first carbon bearing a double bond is number 6 counting from the methyl group. In this book, the formulae and terminology most commonly used will be adopted, for example stearic acid will be specified as C18:0 whereas linoleic acid will be designated as C18:2ω6 and so forth.

TABLE 1

TERMS AND SYMBOLS DESIGNATING FATTY ACIDS IN FOOD OF ANIMAL AND VEGETABLE ORIGIN

Common name	Chain length (number of carbons)	Double bonds (number)	Symbols			Systematic name[1]
			I	II[2]	III[3]	
Butyric	4	0	C4:0		4:0	*n*-Butanoic
Caproic	6	0	C6:0		6:0	*n*-Hexanoic
Caprylic	8	0	C8:0		8:0	*n*-Octanoic
Capric	10	0	C10:0		10:0	*n*-Decanoic
Lauric	12	0	C12:0		12:0	*n*-Dodecanoic
Myristic	14	0	C14:0		14:0	*n*-Tetradecanoic
Palmitic	16	0	C16:0		16:0	*n*-Hexadecanoic
Palmitoleic	16	1	C16:1	C16:1ω7	16:1,n-7	*cis*-9-hexadecenoic
Stearic	18	0	C18:0		18:0	*n*-octadecanoic
Oleic	18	1	C18:1	C18:1ω9	18:1,n-9	*cis*-9-octadecenoic
Linoleic	18	2	C18:2	C18:2ω6	18:2,n-6	*cis, cis*-9,12-octa-decadienoic
γ-Linolenic	18	3	C18:3	C18:3ω6	18:3,n-6	*all cis*-6,9,12-octa-decatrienoic
α-Linolenic	18	3	C18:3	C18:3ω3	18:3,n-3	*all cis*-9,12,15-octa-decatrienoic
Arachidic	20	0	C20:0			*n*-eicosanoic
Gadoleic	20	1	C20:1	C20:1ω9	20:1,n-9	*n*-11-eicosenoic
Arachidonic	20	4	C20:4	C20:4ω6	20:4,n-6	*all cis*-5,8,11,14-eicosatetraenoic
Behenic	22	0	C22:0			*n*-docosanoic
Erucic	22	1	C22:1	C22:1ω9	22:1,n-9	*cis*-13-docosenoic
Clupadonic	22	5	C22:5	C22:5ω3	22:5,n-3	*all cis*-7,10,13,16,19-docosapentaenoic

[1] *Carbon atoms are numbered starting from the carboxyl group which is No. 1. In the case of unsaturated fatty acids, the symbol Δ is sometimes used to indicate points of unsaturation, for example C18:2$\Delta^{9.12}$ for designating linoleic acid, the carboxyl carbon being No. 1*

[2] *Carbon atoms are numbered from the methyl group. The sign ω indicates the first carbon where a point of unsaturation is found*

[3] *The letter "n" gives the position of the first carbon atom where a point of unsaturation is found, starting from the methyl group. The symbols used in this book will be, for example, C18:2, C18:2ω6 or C18:2$\Delta^{9.12}$ for linoleic acid*

It will be noted in Table 1 that the most important fatty acids found naturally in foods of animal or vegetable origin, have carbon chains with an even number of carbon atoms, and that their chain length varies from 4 to 22. Fatty acids having a chain length of 10 carbons or less are sometimes called short-chain fatty acids and they are all saturated. Fatty acids with a chain length of 12 or 14 carbons are medium-chain fatty acids, and those with more than 14 carbons are long chain. Polyunsaturated fatty acids are all long chain.

Chain length and melting point

The chain length of fatty acids is one of the major factors determining the consistency of a food fat at different temperatures. For the saturated fatty acids, it is the only factor. The longer the chain length the higher is the melting point. The following are examples of this phenomenon:

Fatty acid	Symbol	Melting point (°C)
Butyric	C4:0	−7.9
Lauric	C12:0	44.2
Palmitic	C16:0	62.7
Stearic	C18:0	69.6
Arachidic	C20:0	75.4
Behenic	C22:0	80.0

Chain length also affects the melting point of unsaturated fatty acids. For example, the melting point of monounsaturated fatty acids rises from 10.5 to 13.0°C when the chain length increases from C18:1 to C22:1. Chain length of the fatty acids found in foods high in fat may therefore have practical implications in food processing since it is a property that to some extent determines the consistency of the product at a given temperature.

Properties associated with unsaturation

MELTING POINT

The presence of a double bond in a carbon chain of a given length lowers the melting point compared with the corresponding saturated chain. Stearic acid (C18:0), for example, has a melting point of 69.6°C, whereas oleic acid (C18:1) melts at 10.5°C. A second or a third double bond in a chain of similar length would lower the melting point still more. The following are a few examples.

Acid	Symbol	Melting point (°C)
Oleic	C18:1	10.5
Linoleic	C18:2	− 5.0
Linolenic	C18:3	−11.0

ISOMERISM

A double bond in a fatty acid carbon chain permits two possible geometrical arrangements around the point of unsaturation; this phenomenon is called geometrical isomerism, and two types of isomers, *cis* and *trans*, are recognized (Fig 3). In one case, the carbon atoms about the point of unsaturation may be said to adopt a linear configuration to give the *trans* geometrical isomer. In the other case, the carbon atoms take a curved

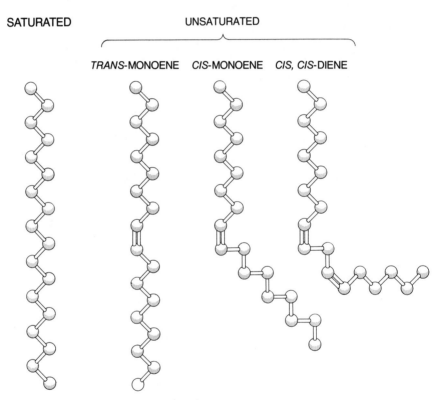

Fig. 3—Schematic illustration of geometrical isomerism found in unsaturated fatty acids.

(Inspired by Spritz and Mishkel[1].)

At the point of unsaturation in unsaturated fatty acids, the carbon atoms with their attached hydrogen atoms may adopt two types of configuration: the *cis* isomers may be said to have a curved configuration, whereas the *trans* isomers have a linear configuration.

configuration to give the *cis* isomer. Geometrical isomerism may be illustrated as in Fig 3.

Unprocessed vegetable oils contain only *cis* isomers: they are curved. Processing these oils in the production of shortenings and margarines may give rise to the formation of large quantities of *trans* isomers. Processing is essential to raise the melting point of the parent oils and to decrease their susceptibility to oxidation and rancidity.

In addition to geometrical isomers, the unsaturated fatty acids may exist in different forms of positional isomers. The positional isomers have their double bond or bonds at different positions on the carbon chain. For example elaidic acid, a fatty acid with one double bond of the *trans* configuration in position 9 (*trans*-C18:1Δ^9), becomes vaccenic acid if the double bond migrates to position 11 (*trans*-C18:1Δ^{11}). The processing of vegetable oils in the production of shortenings and margarines also causes the formation of positional isomers. This phenomenon will be discussed more fully in Chapter 3.

PEROXIDATION

A double bond in the carbon chain of unsaturated fatty acids makes them susceptible to oxidation and peroxidation reactions. Oxidation and peroxidation occur externally, that is outside the body, in the presence of atmospheric oxygen, and internally within the body, in the presence of respiratory oxygen. Peroxidation reactions are extremely complex and lead to the formation of various by-products, the first of these being free radicals which are unstable and cause instability within the fatty acid molecules (Fig 4). Various re-arrangements take place within the molecule and many new substances are formed, such as alcohols, ketones or aldehydes. These substances are responsible for the bad odor and unpleasant taste of rancid fats and oils.

The chemical reactions involved in the formation of free radicals and peroxides are numerous. They may be the result of auto-oxidation, which occurs naturally in oils rich in polyunsaturated fatty acids, or they may be catalyzed by specific enzymes present in the oils.

Polyunsaturated fatty acids are particularly susceptible to oxidation so that natural or synthetic anti-oxidants are essential for the preservation of foods high in such acids. The living cell may also be exposed to many kinds of peroxidation reaction due to the presence of polyunsaturated fatty acids. The free radicals which are formed during peroxidation reactions are similar to those formed during exposure to radioactivity. Therefore they represent a danger to all human cells which must be constantly protected by natural anti-oxidants. Vitamin E is a natural anti-oxidant and is highly effective.

Peroxidation reactions associated with polyunsaturated fatty acids therefore constitute a hazard in the food industry as well as in the living

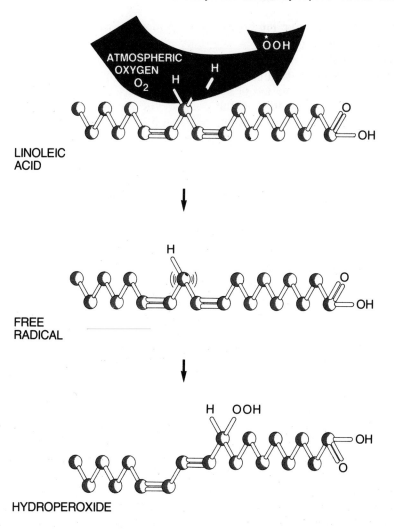

LINOLEIC
ACID

FREE
RADICAL

HYDROPEROXIDE

Fig. 4—Sequence of events associated with the peroxidation of polyunsaturated fatty acids.

(Inspired by Gurr and James[2].)

Polyunsaturated fatty acids are susceptible to oxidation in the presence of oxygen in the air or from respiration. Free radicals are formed: unstable products that result in molecular imbalance culminating in the formation of endoperoxides, peroxides, ketones, aldehydes, alcohols and other products. Rancidity is a manifestation of the oxidation of unsaturated fatty acids. Natural or synthetic antioxidants protect foodstuffs and living cells against these reactions.

cell. Natural or synthetic anti-oxidants are the substances which protect us against these undesirable reactions. Partial hydrogenation used in the processing of vegetable oils, as will be discussed in Chapter 3, reduces the content of polyunsaturated fatty acids in the treated oil and diminishes the risk of peroxidation in foods containing vegetable oils.

GLYCERIDES

Dietary fats contain practically no free fatty acids; instead these are present in the form of triglycerides consisting of one molecule of glycerol and three molecules of fatty acid. Glycerol is a three-carbon atom chain with one hydroxyl group (—OH) on each of the carbon atoms. These hydroxyl groups react with the carboxyl groups (—COOH) of three fatty acids to form a tri-ester molecule.

An illustration of such a triglyceride molecule is presented in Fig 5. It is seen that the three positions (α, β, α') on the glycerol molecule are occupied by three fatty acids (R_1, R_2, R_3). If only two positions were occupied by fatty acids the molecule would be a diglyceride, and a mono-

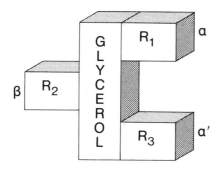

Fig. 5—Schematic illustration of a triglyceride.

Dietary fats and fat in adipose tissue are mixed triglycerides. The fatty acids on the glycerol molecule may differ in carbon chain length and/or in the number of double bonds for each of the positions. Saturated fats contain a great proportion of saturated fatty acids, while unsaturated fats contain a high proportion of polyunsaturated fatty acids.

glyceride in the case where only one position were occupied by a fatty acid. In monoglycerides and diglycerides the free hydroxyl groups (—OH) retain their original properties.

Dietary fats and depot fats in humans and animals are mixed triglycerides, which means that the three positions are occupied by different fatty acids. In the laboratory, however, it is possible to prepare triglycerides in which the three positions are occupied by the same type of fatty acid. For instance, synthetic triolein is made of one molecule of glycerol on which each of the three positions is occupied by oleic acid.

Natural fats and oils consist of mixed triglycerides only. As there are three positions on the glycerol molecule and at least twenty different fatty acids, one can realize the great number of chemically different triglycerides that could be found in food fats as well as in human fats. For example, one could formulate at least 15 different triglycerides when three fatty acids such as palmitic, oleic and stearic acids are used. These 15 triglycerides moreover would have different physical and physiological properties. This is indicative of the great variety in the composition of the triglycerides found in foods and in depot fats.

The fatty acid distribution on the glycerol molecules in nature does not occur by chance. It is now known that, for certain types of fats, there is a preference for certain fatty acids to occupy positions α, β or α'. In milk fat, for example, the long-chain saturated fatty acids tend to be localized in the α position whereas the short-chain fatty acids are found in the α' position (Table 2). Intermediate-chain saturated fatty acids are found mainly in the β position. In this way, butyric acid (C4:0) in cow's milk is found mainly in the α' position and stearic acid (C18:0) in the α position. In human milk, unsaturated acids occupy mainly the α and α' positions.

TABLE 2

POSITION OF THE MAJOR FATTY ACIDS IN MILK-FAT TRIGLYCERIDES*[1]

Position	C4:0	C6:0	C8:0	C10:0	C12:0	C14:0	C16:0	C18:0	C18:1	C18:2
HUMAN MILK										
α					1	3	16	15	46	11
β					2	7	58	3	13	7
α'				2	6	7	6	2	50	15
COW'S MILK										
α	5	3	1	3	3	11	36	15	21	1
β	3	5	2	6	6	20	33	6	14	3
α'	43	11	2	4	4	7	10	4	15	1

* Adapted from Breckenridge[3] and Breckenridge, Marai and Kuksis[4]
[1] Expressed in molecular percentage for a given position

In fats of animal origin the saturated fatty acids palmitic (C16:0) and stearic (C18:0) are found mainly in the α and α' positions. There is a notable exception, however, in pork fat where palmitic acid (C16:0) is primarily located in the β position. Unsaturated fatty acids in the depot fats of both man and cattle preferentially occupy the β position. In pork they are found in large proportions in the α and α' positions.

In vegetable oils, about 70 per cent of the linoleic acid (C18:2ω6) content occupies the β position while the saturated fatty acids occupy the α and α' positions. In coconut oil, which contains a high proportion of short-chain and medium-chain acids, the distribution of the different saturated fatty acids resembles that of milk fat.

The position of the particular fatty acids in triglycerides is of significance during the digestion and absorption of fats when monoglycerides and diglycerides are formed. It is of significance also during the formation of phospholipids in the body, where enzyme activity is specific for the different positions on the glycerol molecule. The fact that polyunsaturated fatty acids of vegetable oils are found predominantly in the β position will have some significance in the metabolism of *trans* fatty acids appearing in partially hydrogenated oils used in the fabrication of shortenings and margarines. This will be discussed later.

PHOSPHOLIPIDS

Phospholipids, diesters of phosphoric acid, constitute an important group of lipidic compounds. Fig 6 illustrates one molecule of phosphoric acid: note the two hydroxyl groups (—OH) which form esters with different compounds to form the phospholipids.

Fig. 6—Schematic illustration of phosphoric acid, the basic molecule in the formation of phospholipids.

Phospholipids are diesters of phosphoric acid. Their physiological and metabolic functions in the organism are extremely varied and their molecular structure is complex. Note the two hydroxyl groups where reactions take place with other molecules to yield phospholipids.

Phosphoglycerides

A great proportion of the phospholipids found in animals and in plants belong to the family of phosphoglycerides. Their nomenclature is based on the particular molecules which are linked to the phosphoric acid molecule. As seen in Fig 6 there are two positions (X_1, and X_2) on the phosphoric acid molecule that may react with other molecules. For many phospholipids, position X_1 is esterified with one hydroxyl group of glycerol to give the basic molecule of the phosphoglyceride family.

On the other hand, position X_2 of phosphoric acid may react with the hydroxyl group of other molecules, as, for example, of choline, serine or inositol. Fig. 7 gives an illustration of the composition of different types of phosphoglycerides.

Phosphoglycerides are the commonest of all phospholipids and are found in both animals and plants. The soybean lecithins, for example,

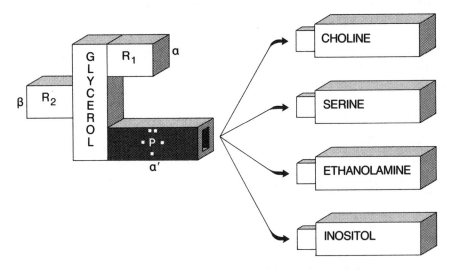

Fig. 7—Schematic illustration of some phosphoglycerides.

A great proportion of the phospholipids both in animals and plants belong to the phosphoglyceride family. Their nomenclature is based on the particular molecules which are esterified with phosphoric acid. They are called phosphatidylcholine, phosphatidylserine, phosphatidylethanolamine or phosphatidylinositol depending on whether choline, serine, ethanolamine or inositol are part of the molecule. Lecithins are phosphatidyl cholines. The nature of the fatty acids R_1 and R_2 in the α or β positions, respectively, gives the different phospholipids their particular physical and physiological properties.

belong to the phosphatidylcholine family and are important emulsifying agents used in the industrial preparation of many foods rich in fat.

Note that, in general, the fatty acid R_2 in the β position is an unsaturated fatty acid, oleic acid, linoleic acid or arachidonic acid. Most of the time, the fatty acid in the α position is saturated.

Sphingolipids

Instead of reacting with glycerol, the X_1 group of phosphoric acid (Fig 6) may form an ester with the terminal hydroxyl group (—OH) of sphingosine to give a sphingolipid. Sphingosine[5] has a chain of 18 carbon atoms on which are found a *trans* double bond, two hydroxyl groups and one amino group (—NH$_2$). In this case, the X_2 group of phosphoric acid is esterified with the hydroxyl group of choline.

Sphinogomyelins are important components of the myelin sheath which surrounds nerve axons. In this case, a long-chain fatty acid is coupled to the amino group (—NH$_2$) of sphingosine. Fig 8 shows a sphingomyelin molecule.

The main difference between the various sphingomyelins lies in the nature of the fatty acid R, which may have a chain length of from 16 to 24 carbon atoms. Lignoceric acid (C24:0) and nervonic acid (C24:1) are abundant[5]. The brain is rich in sphingolipids and in sphingomyelin in par-

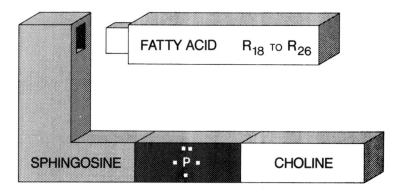

Fig. 8—Schematic illustration of a sphingomyelin molecule.

Sphingomyelins are important constituents of the myelin sheath which surrounds nerve axons. The fatty acids R which are part of these molecules are long-chain fatty acids —18 to 26 carbon atoms. Both the chain length and degree of saturation of the fatty acid R may alter the physical and physiological properties of these substances.

ticular. The nature of the fats consumed may influence the ratio of the different fatty acids incorporated in the different sphingolipids of the body. The physiological consequences of this influence, however, are still unknown.

GLYCOLIPIDS

Cerebrosides

Cerebrosides such as sphingomyelins contain one sphingosine molecule, but neither phosphoric acid nor choline. Instead, a sugar-like molecule, or more correctly a galactose-like molecule, is attached to the sphingosine (Fig 9). Cerebrosides are also important constituents of the myelin sheath surrounding the nerve axons. The fatty acid R is always a long-chain fatty acid; stearic acid (C18:0) is predominant[5].

Gangliosides

Gangliosides are compounds which, like cerebrosides, contain one molecule of sphingosine, but the galactose-like component is a complex carbohydrate. Fig 10 is an illustration of a ganglioside. The gray matter of the brain is rich in gangliosides.

CHOLESTEROL AND OTHER STEROIDS

Cholesterol is a lipidic compound found in every cell in the human body; its physiological functions are numerous. The fact that cholesterol is found to accumulate in atheroma, in gallstones and in renal calculi (all disease conditions), should not overshadow the essential functions of this substance in the body. It is necessary, therefore, to know what cholesterol is, to know some of its physical and physiological properties, and to understand properly the multiple functions it serves in the human body.

An illustration of the cholesterol molecule is presented in Fig 11. Note that carbon and hydrogen are the main constituents of cholesterol, and that carbon atoms are linked to one another to form four rings designated by the letters A, B, C and D. Note also the numbering system adopted by chemists to identify each carbon.

The hydroxyl group on carbon 3 and the four rings A, B, C and D of the cholesterol molecule are also the basic structure of an important group of compounds known as the steroids. Cholesterol is only one of numerous steroids found in the human body and in dietary fats. Steroids in foods of vegetable origin are sometimes known as phytosterols.

Cholesterol is practically insoluble in water. This property is the basis of the numerous and vital functions of cholesterol in the body. This property is also the cause of the difficulties encountered in the handling of cholesterol by the human body which is essentially an aqueous milieu. That is why the transport of cholesterol in blood, or in extracellular and intracellular fluids, requires specially adapted and complex mechanisms. Because it is insoluble in water, cholesterol is prone to accumulate as calculi, for example in gallstones, and in lipid plaques on the intima of the arteries.

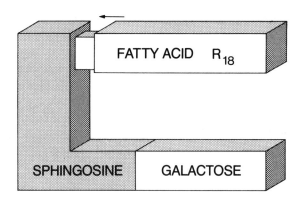

Fig. 9—Schematic illustration of a cerebroside.

Cerebrosides are constituents of the myelin sheath of the nerve axons. Stearic acid (C18:0) is the predominant fatty acid R.

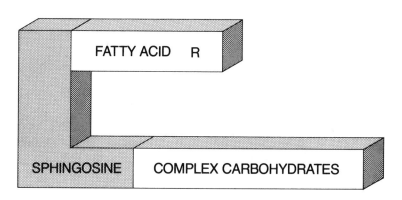

Fig. 10—Schematic illustration of a ganglioside.

Gangliosides are lipid compounds containing fatty acids, complex carbohydrates and sphingosine. The gray matter of the brain is rich in gangliosides. The nature of the constituent fatty acid R can be influenced by the type of fat consumed in the diet, but the physiological consequences of such a change are not well understood.

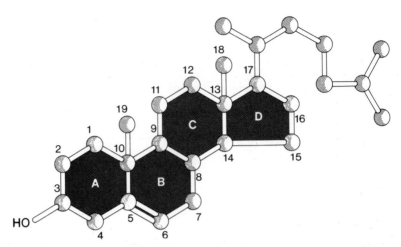

Fig. 11—Schematic illustration of the cholesterol molecule.

The cholesterol molecule contains mainly carbon and hydrogen. The carbon atoms are linked to one another to form four rings designated as rings A, B, C and D. There is a hydroxyl group on carbon 3 (Ring A) which reacts with fatty acids to form cholesterol esters. Both cholesterol and cholesterol esters are practically insoluble in water and body fluids. Cholesterol and its fatty acid esters are essential for the proper functioning of body cells.

The hydroxyl group (—OH) on carbon 3, ring A, gives cholesterol the ability to form esters with fatty acids. Fig 12 gives an example of such an ester where linoleic acid (C18:2ω6) is reacted with cholesterol. Cholesterol in the body is found mainly in the form of cholesterol esters.

The solubility of these esters in water or in body fluids differs greatly depending on the nature of the fatty acid with which cholesterol is esterified. Their solubility presumably has a bearing on the atherogenicity of cholesterol esters. Thus, the esters of monounsaturated fatty acids might be expected to be more atherogenic than esters of saturated fatty acids. Linoleic (C18:2ω6), linolenic (C18:2ω3) and arachidonic acid (C20:4ω6) esters, correspondingly, would be less atherogenic than esters of monounsaturated or saturated fatty acids[6].

Cholesterol is the precursor of many steroids synthesized in the human body. The diversity of the molecules of which cholesterol is the parent substance is apparent in Fig 13. These molecules play vital roles in the liver, adrenal glands, skin and sex organs.

Among the most important derivatives of cholesterol are the bile acids which originate in the liver and play a major role in the digestion of fats

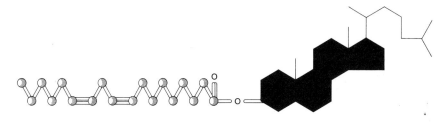

Fig. 12—Schematic illustration of a cholesterol ester.

Cholesterol esters are vital constituents of all cells in the human body. Their low solubility in body fluids creates difficulties associated with their transport and explains why they are prone to form deposits in certain tissues. The nature of dietary fats changes the ratio of the various fatty acids which undergo esterification with cholesterol within the body. The consequences of these changes on health are being studied.

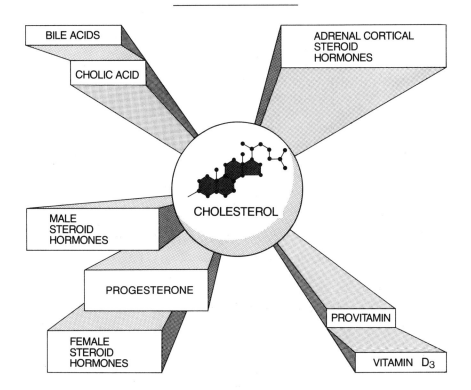

Fig. 13—Some derivatives of cholesterol.

Cholesterol is the precursor of many substances essential to life, such as bile acids, hormones and vitamin D_3. All body cells must be constantly supplied with cholesterol. This is ensured by a supply from the diet or by its biosynthesis in the liver.

after being secreted into the intestinal tract; equally noteworthy is the derivative 7-dehydrocholesterol, which gives vitamin D_3 under the action of ultraviolet radiation from the sun. Other derivatives are the male and female sex hormones and the steroid hormones synthesized by the adrenal glands. The numerous physiological and metabolic functions of these substances are all essential to life.

In addition, cholesterol is essential for the formation of cell membranes and for the maintenance of their integrity. The body cells could not reproduce, grow or function normally if they were not constantly supplied with cholesterol. The human body therefore depends on specialized mechanisms governing and maintaining cholesterol homeostasis essential for proper body function. Some of these mechanisms involve the synthesis of cholesterol in the liver, excretion in the intestine and feedback reactions.

BILE ACIDS

Bile acids are synthesized in the liver from cholesterol. The main intermediate product is cholic acid which reacts with glycine or taurine to give the bile acids, glycocholic and taurocholic acids, respectively. Fig 14 shows the relationship between these substances[5]. The bile acids in turn, react with sodium or potassium present in bile to give the bile salts[7].

It is known that the enzymes in tissue cells are unable to break down the steroid nucleus, the core of the cholesterol molecule. Bile acids are therefore the final products of cholesterol metabolism and constitute the principal way cholesterol is eliminated from the body.

Bile, in addition to bile salts, contains approximately 1 per cent cholesterol. This free cholesterol is incorporated into micelles which are formed between bile salts and bile phospholipids. At this concentration, however, cholesterol is near the threshold of insolubility: any disorder will lead to the formation of calculi. The bile is obviously the major pathway, if not the only one, through which cholesterol is eliminated from the body. Once it is secreted into the intestine, cholesterol may be reabsorbed to become available again for the different roles it plays.

In humans, 20–30 grams of bile acids are secreted each day into the intestine via the bile duct[5]. The major part, perhaps 90 per cent, is reabsorbed, returns to the liver and is re-utilized. This cycle is called the enterohepatic cycle. It is remarkably efficient as bile acids can be re-utilized 6–10 times daily with a loss of only 200–500 mg for a total of 3,000–5,000 mg produced—a loss of roughly 10 per cent.

The efficacy of the enterohepatic circulation contributes greatly to reducing the rate at which cholesterol is eliminated from the body. Certain drugs and certain dietary fibers accelerate the elimination of cholesterol by inhibiting the reabsorption of bile salts from the intestine and in this

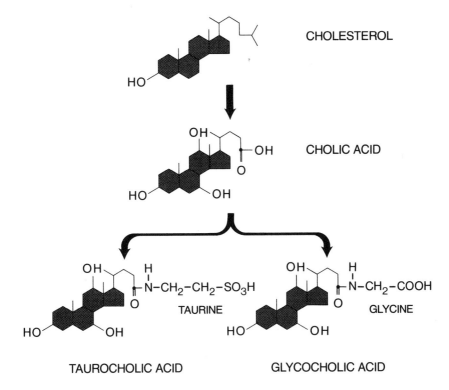

Fig. 14—Formation of bile acids from cholesterol.

Cholesterol is the parent substance in the formation of bile acids and bile salts. Bile salts help in the digestion of fats, first as emulsifiers and then as part of the micelles which are formed with the products of fat digestion and other lipidic compounds present in the intestinal tract. Part of the bile acids is reabsorbed and reutilized; the rest is excreted via the feces. The formation of bile acids and their excretion into the intestinal tract and ultimately the feces constitutes the main pathway through which cholesterol is eliminated from the body.

way reduce the efficacy of the enterohepatic circulation. The enterohepatic circulation could therefore be considered as one of those special mechanisms that help to maintain cholesterol homeostasis.

Bile salts, because of their composition and polarity, have the ability to decrease considerably the surface tension of water and consequently to promote the emulsification of fats present in the intestine. The resulting formation of small fat-droplets is an important step in their digestion. The

bile salts are also responsible for the formation of water-soluble aggregates—such as micelles—containing the products of the digestion of dietary fats, fatty acids, monoglycerides and so forth. These micelles are the
principal form in which the final products of fat digestion are absorbed at
the level of the brush border of the intestinal villi. Phenomena associated
with the digestion and absorption of fats have been described in detail by
many authors[8-10]

LIPOPROTEINS

Fatty acids, phospholipids, cholesterol and other lipids are all practically insoluble in water. Their transport in blood and extracellular fluids
therefore requires special mechanisms. Thus, triglycerides, phospholipids
and free or esterified cholesterol, in transit from the sites of absorption to
the sites of utilization, or from the sites of degradation to the sites of
elimination, are always associated with proteins with which they form
globular aggregates, which in turn react like soluble compounds.

The formation of these aggregates is based on the polarity rather than
on the chemical properties of each constituent molecule. Polarity is a
physicochemical property governing the behavior of various molecules in
aqueous solution. It is caused by the presence or absence of electrical
charges localized at given points on a molecule. Water (H_2O) is a polar
compound because the negatively charged oxygen atom attracts the slightly
positively charged hydrogen atom of another water molecule. A particular
O—H– – – – –O bridge is formed between water molecules, and this affinity
determines the orientation and the interrelation of these molecules in their
milieu[2]. Highly polarized compounds are soluble in water and are said to
be hydrophilic. In contrast, non-polar compounds have no electrical
charges on any part of the molecule and are insoluble in water. These
compounds are said to be hydrophobic.

This phenomenon explains why fatty acids, triglycerides, cholesterol
and other lipid molecules are insoluble in water. These compounds have
many carbon to carbon (—C—C) or carbon to hydrogen (—C—H) linkages
which do not lead to the emergence of positive or negative charges on their
molecules.

With respect to polarity, phospholipids are of special interest. The
phosphate group is negatively charged, whereas choline, serine and ethanolamine, which react with the phosphate group, are positively charged
because of the nitrogen they contain. Phospholipids are therefore highly
polar. In an aqueous milieu, as that of the human body, they tend to be
oriented in such a way that their polar points are bound as strongly as
possible to the surrounding aqueous milieu, while their non-polar *tails* tend

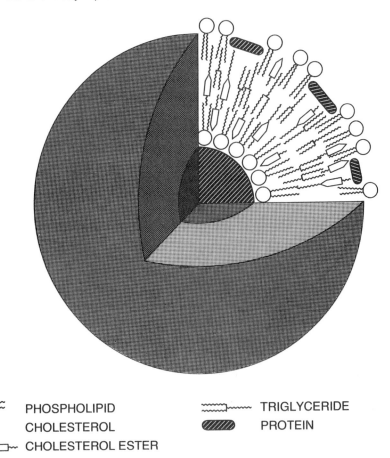

O~~~ PHOSPHOLIPID   ~~~⊐~~~ TRIGLYCERIDE
◁⊐~   CHOLESTEROL   ▨▨▨   PROTEIN
~~◁⊐~ CHOLESTEROL ESTER

Fig. 15—*A schematic illustration of a lipoprotein complex.*

(Inspired by Finer *et al*[11].)

Lipoproteins may be represented as microspheres consisting of
proteins, phospholipids and free and esterified cholesterol; the
relationship between these compounds within the microspheres
is governed by their respective polarities. Lipoproteins are the
major carriers of lipids in the bloodstream. They are generally
classified according to their density as VLDL (Very Low Density
Lipoproteins), LDL (Low Density Lipoproteins) and HDL (High
Density Lipoproteins). The protein fraction has the property of
controlling the activity of certain enzymes, as for example the
lipoprotein lipase. Lipoproteins are currently the object of inten-
sive research.

to coalesce in the same area. This is a key phenomenon in the formation of micelles, membranes, lipoproteins and similar structures.

A model of a lipoprotein is shown in Fig 15. The lipid components[11] are distributed in three more or less distinct layers around the protein core with which they are associated. The orientation of the phospholipid molecules between the protein component and the ambient water milieu is governed by their respective polarities. The less polarized compounds, like free and esterified cholesterol and triglycerides, are aligned in such a way that their fatty acids are oriented toward the layer where the least polarized points of the molecules are found[11]. The term lipoprotein is generally applied to these aggregates which are the form in which triglycerides, phospholipids and free or esterified cholesterol are transported in the body.

Historical

Marcheboeuf in 1929[12,13] showed that lipids in the blood serum are closely associated with protein fractions, but it was only in the 1950s that there arose an interest in these particular protein complexes which gradually became to be known as the *lipoproteins*. During that period, new techniques based on ultracentrifugation and paper electrophoresis made it possible to separate and identify the different lipoproteins. At that time researchers began to suspect a relationship between a high level of lipoproteins in blood plasma and premature coronary heart disease in certain subjects[14]. It was learned later[15] that serum lipids, with the exception of free fatty acids, are transported in the form of these macromolecular complexes. During the same period, three different types of protein were identified as being components of lipoproteins; these were given the name apolipoproteins.

The scientific information concerning lipoproteins found application in the field of human health during the 1960s when Fredrickson, Levy and Lees[16-19] associated the different lipoproteins with different physiological functions. Based on the composition of serum lipoproteins, they suggested five different phenotypes of hyperlipoproteinemia. Fredrickson's classification became commonly—if not universally—used for distinguishing hyperlipemic conditions in man.

Classification

Lipoproteins, which include also chylomicrons, are subdivided into five main categories. The chylomicrons are formed in the intestinal mucosa mainly from products of the absorption of digested dietary fats. From the intestinal mucosa they enter the lymph circulation to be discharged into the peripheral blood at the level of the left subclavian vein. The true lipoproteins have different points of origin and are found in the blood stream.

Chylomicrons and lipoproteins of all categories, as mentioned previously, consist mainly of proteins, triglycerides, phospholipids and free and esterified cholesterol. Their respective content of lipid and the particular composition of their apolipoproteins form the basis for the classification of lipoproteins. The lipoproteins high in triglycerides (*see* Fig 5) have a lower density than those high in proteins and low in triglycerides. Using ultracentrifugation techniques it is possible to separate the different types of lipoproteins according to their density.

It is also possible to separate the different types of lipoproteins on the basis of their constituent apolipoproteins, using electrophoretic techniques. In this way, proteins in solution can be effectively separated according to their respective rate of migration in an electric field. Ultracentrifugation and electrophoresis are therefore the two methods used regularly to separate, identify and study the different types of lipoproteins circulating in blood.

A few of the physical characteristics used to identify and classify the different types of lipoproteins are shown in Table 3. Chylomicrons are the largest globules having a diameter of 300–5,000 Å. They are also the lightest, their density being less than 0.95 g/ml.

The other types of lipoproteins are classified according to increasing density and decreasing size. They are classified as follows:

VLDL (*Very Low Density Lipoproteins*)
IDL (*Intermediate Density Lipoproteins*)
LDL (*Low Density Lipoproteins*)
HDL (*High Density Lipoproteins*)

With regard to HDL, there is a tendency to distinguish between HDL_2 and HDL_3. Some authors even add a new category, VHDL (Very High Density Lipoproteins) the density of which ranges from 1.21 to 1.25 g/ml. Thus chylomicrons and VLDL represent the largest lipoprotein globules and also the lightest, while HDL represent the smallest and the heaviest.

A gradual increase in the density of lipoproteins is accompanied by a corresponding decrease in the triglyceride content on the one hand and an increase in the protein content, on the other (Table 4). Thus chylomicrons contain approximately 87 per cent triglycerides while HDL contain no more than 6–7 percent. The triglyceride composition of the other types of lipoproteins is intermediate. Conversely, the protein or apolipoprotein content rises from 2 per cent in chylomicrons to approximately 50 per cent in HDL. The concentration of phospholipids varies inversely as that of the triglycerides, from chylomicrons to HDL. It is to be noted that IDL and LDL have the highest concentrations of cholesterol.

In a final analysis, it would appear that the classification of lipoproteins as shown in Tables 3 and 4 is somewhat artificial. In fact, the classification into five categories is based on no more than minute differences. Indeed, one could easily imagine that these tiny globules of lipids and proteins are chylomicrons, changing in size and density as triglycerides leave to become an immediate source of cellular energy or to be deposited in the adipose tissue as a future source of energy. The roles of each category of lipoproteins in the transport and metabolism of dietary or endogenous lipids are described in Chapter 6.

TABLE 3

SOME PHYSICAL CHARACTERISTICS USED TO IDENTIFY AND CLASSIFY THE DIFFERENT TYPES OF LIPOPROTEINS*

Classification	Abbreviated name	Other terms	Density (g/ml)	Dimensions	Flotation index
Chylomicrons	–	–	< 0.950	300–5,000 Å	> 400
Very Low Density Lipoproteins	VLDL	Pre-beta-lipoproteins	0.950–1.006	280–1,000 Å	20–400
Intermediate Density Lipoproteins	IDL	Beta-lipoproteins	1.006–1.019	250– 300 Å	12–20
Low Density Lipoproteins	LDL	Beta-lipoproteins	1.019–1.063	200– 250 Å	0–12
High Density Lipoproteins	HDL$_2$ HDL$_3$	Alpha-lipoproteins	1.063–1.12 1.12–1.21	90– 120 Å	Do not float
Very High Density Lipoproteins	VHDL		1.21–1.25		

* Data taken from references[9,16,20–22]

$$\overset{\circ}{A} = \frac{1}{10,000} \, micron$$

TABLE 4

COMPOSITION OF THE DIFFERENT TYPES OF LIPOPROTEINS (%)*

Classification	Total proteins	Total lipids	Triglyc-erides	Phospho-lipids	Cholesterol		
					Free	Esterified	Total
Chylomicrons	2	98	84	8	2	4	6
VLDL	9	91	56	15	5	15	20
IDL	16	84	30	14	9	31	40
LDL	23	77	9	22	8	38	46
HDL	48	52	6	26	5	15	20

* Based on references[2,9,16,17,20–24]

Apolipoproteins

The apolipoproteins are the protein components of lipoproteins. The nature of these proteins is varied and has been studied extensively. For many apolipoproteins the sequence of their amino acids, their molecular weight and some of their physiological and biochemical functions are known[9,20-22,25]. By convention, these apolipoproteins are identified by the letters A, B, C, D and E[26]. Each letter represents more than one protein and so refers to a family of apolipoproteins rather than to one well defined type of protein molecule.

The apolipoproteins in each category of lipoproteins are identified in Table 5. Chylomicrons and VLDL are rich in Apo A, Apo B and Apo C, whereas, IDL and LDL for all practical purposes contain only Apo B. HDL are characterized mainly by their content of Apo A.

TABLE 5

APOLIPOPROTEINS OF THE DIFFERENT TYPES OF LIPOPROTEINS*

	Chylomicrons	VLDL	IDL	LDL	HDL
Major apolipoproteins	Apo A–I Apo B Apo C	Apo B Apo C–I[1] Apo C–II[2] Apo C–III[3] Apo E[4]	Apo B	Apo B	Apo A–I Apo A–II
Minor apolipoproteins	Apo A–II Apo E	Apo A–I Apo A–II Apo D	Apo C–I[1] Apo C–II[2] Apo C–III[3] Apo E[4]		Apo C–I[1] Apo C–II[2] Apo C–III[3] Apo D(Apo A–III) Apo E[4]

* Based on references[9,20,21,25]
[1] High in serine
[2] High in glutamic acid
[3] High in alanine
[4] High in arginine

The chain length of the peptides and their amino acids content are the main characteristics used to distinguish between the different families of apolipoproteins or between members of the same family. Thus Apo C-I is the smallest of the apolipoproteins and contains only 57 amino acids, while Apo C-II, a member of the same family, contains 100. Apo A-I, as another example, contains 245 amino acids and has a molecular weight of 27,000 to 28,000, while Apo A-II consists of two chains of 77 amino acids bridged by the sulphur-containing amino acid, cystine[9,20].

In summary, the apolipoproteins are synthesized partly by the intestine and partly by the liver. Their main function is to form macromolecular complexes with triglycerides, phospholipids and free and esterified cholesterol and, in this way, serve as carriers for these lipids in blood and other body fluids (*see* Fig 15). In addition, some apolipoproteins can activate or inhibit certain enzymes involved in the metabolism of lipids (*see* Chapter 6).

PROSTAGLANDINS

Life is the result of an extremely complex equilibrium within each cell and each tissue, between myriads of chemical reactions oriented in one direction or another by messenger molecules. Some of these molecules are short lived and appear or disappear quickly depending upon the needs of the entire body. Prostaglandins are such molecules: they initiate or inhibit special enzymatic processes within the body cells which enable the body to react against the insults of its environment and in this way to maintain its living functions. Unlike hormones, which are synthesized by specific glands and transported in blood to the site of their action, prostaglandins are generally synthesized *in situ* and catabolized quickly so that their activity is potent but transient.

The prostaglandins are lipidic substances isolated for the first time by Bergström and Sjövell[27] from sheep sex glands and their secretions. The term prostaglandin was coined by van Euler who thought they originated from the prostate. It is now known that the prostaglandins in mammals are synthesized not only by the seminal vesicles but also by many other organs and tissues including kidney, lung, thymus, spleen, iris, thyroid, adipose tissue, uterus, placenta, intestinal mucosa, adrenal gland and ovary. The ubiquity of prostaglandins as well as the diversity of their functions and structures is remarkable.

The prostaglandins are elaborated in the body cells from polyunsaturated fatty acids, linoleic acid ($C18:2\omega6$) and arachidonic acid ($C20:4\omega6$). At least sixteen different prostaglandins are presently known[28,29] and they are classified in two different series: the PG_1 and PG_2. The PG_1 series is derived from linoleic acid and the PG_2 series from arachidonic acid. Fig 16 shows some prostaglandins of the PG_2 series. The prostaglandins of the PG_1 series, derived from linoleic acid[29], have no double bond between carbons 5 and 6 from the carboxyl group.

In the body cells, the polyunsaturated fatty acids which are needed for the synthesis of prostaglandins are supplied by the phospholipids. When these fatty acids are needed for the synthesis of prostaglandins, a special enzyme, phospholipase A, catalyzes the detachment of the required polyunsaturated acid. For this, however, the required fatty acid must be in the β position on the phospholipid molecule (Fig 7).

As mentioned above, the physiological functions of prostaglandins are numerous and extremely diversified. To attempt to give an accurate and complete classification of these functions would be a daring undertaking. Suffice to describe briefly one of their functions in lipid metabolism. The adipose tissue, as is well known, constitutes the most important reserve of energy in the body. When energy is needed, certain hormones such as adrenalin, noradrenalin and ACTH[29] induce the liberation of fatty acids

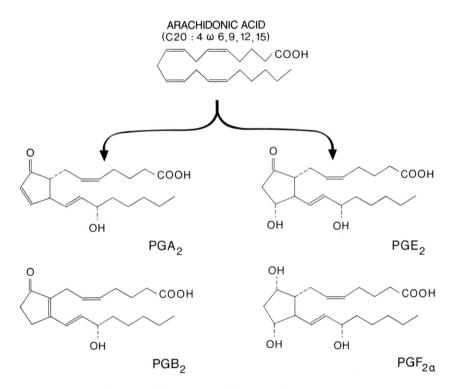

Fig. 16—*Schematic illustration of prostaglandins of the series PG$_2$.*

(Inspired by Curtis-Prior[29].)

The prostaglandins are derivatives of the polyunsaturated linoleic and arachidonic acids. They are synthesized *in situ* and are catabolized quickly. Their physiological functions are numerous and extremely diversified. Their activity takes place in the adipose tissue, the digestive system, the circulatory system, the nervous system and in many inflammatory reactions.

from the stored triglycerides. The freed fatty acids enter the blood stream and are used by the particular tissues in need of energy. Simultaneously, prostaglandins of the PG_1 series are synthesized in the adipose tissue itself and the activity of the lipolytic hormones mentioned above is gradually inhibited. Without this inhibitory action of the prostaglandins, the lipolytic hormones could eventually cause the complete lysis of the adipose tissue. The delicate balance between the activity of the lipolytic hormones causing the hydrolysis of triglycerides and that of the specialized prostaglandins inhibiting lipolysis is therefore essential to maintain the homeostasis of the adipose tissue and to ensure the availability of energy for every cell of the body when needed.

On the other hand, a fault in the sequence of events that govern the production of PG_1 prostaglandins would lead to pathological changes in the adipose tissue. In fact, certain cases of obesity of metabolic origin can be explained by an excessive production of PG_1 prostaglandins. In such cases, an excessive inhibition of the events governing the hydrolysis of triglycerides stored in the adipose tissue can be observed. As a result, the fat deposited remains captive in the adipocytes and obesity sets in. The organism must then draw its energy from blood glucose and from hepatic and muscular glycogen. As these sources of energy are rapidly exhausted, this phenomenon could explain the apparent lethargy of the obese[29].

Under these conditions, a plausible therapy could be the use of drugs capable of decreasing the production of prostaglandins or of inhibiting their activity in the adipose tissue itself. Unfortunately this practice would be difficult, if not dangerous. Since prostaglandins are normally synthesized at their site of action and are quickly catabolized, they do not always enter into the blood circulation to be transported to other sites. Furthermore, their activity may be different from one tissue or organ to another. Consequently, attempting to modify lipid metabolism in the obese through the use of prostaglandins would be accompanied by unforeseeable risks.

At this point, it is essential to mention recent work[30] which indicates that the inhibiting activity attributed to the PG_1 prostaglandins might in fact be due to endoperoxides which are transient intermediate compounds produced during the synthesis of prostaglandins. The thromboxanes are among these intermediate products. Polyunsaturated fatty acids are the precursors of endoperoxides, thromboxanes and prostaglandins. It will be some time, however, before the respective roles of prostaglandins, endoperoxides and thromboxanes in the human body are elucidated.

Prostaglandins have other physiological functions in the reproductive, digestive, circulatory and nervous systems and in inflammatory reactions. The interested reader is invited to refer to the references quoted in this chapter for additional information on the subject of endoperoxides, thromboxanes and prostaglandins.

CONCLUSION

Dietary fats and body lipids are varied in nature and sometimes extremely complex. We have only described in this chapter the lipidic compounds which will be referred to later in the book and about which the reader may care to be reminded. Indeed there are other lipidic substances which are essential for health, for example the lipid-soluble vitamins, the essential fatty acids, certain hormones, and others, but the reader, if he wishes, may obtain the necessary information on these from the references given at the end of this chapter.

We believe it is essential to draw attention to the molecular structure of a certain number of lipidic compounds and to recall briefly some of their properties, so as to understand better their respective role and behavior in both the human body and the food industry. An understanding of the phenomena presented in the following chapters depends largely on the information the reader will find in this chapter.

REFERENCES

1. Spritz N, Mishkel MA: Effects of dietary fats on plasma lipids and lipoproteins: an hypothesis for the lipid-lowering effect of unsaturated fatty acids. J Clin Invest, 48:78–86, 1969

2. Gurr MI, James AT: Lipid Biochemistry: an introduction (ed 2). London, Chapman and Hall, 1975

3. Breckenridge WC: Stereospecific analysis of triacylglycerols. In Kuksis A (ed) Handbook of Lipid Research, vol 1, Fatty Acids and Glycerides, pp 197–232. New York, Plenum Press, 1978

4. Breckenridge WC, Marai L, Kuksis A: Triglyceride structure of human milk fat. Can J Biochem, 47:761–769, 1969

5. Karlson P: Biochimie (ed 2). Paris, Doin, 1971

6. Krumdieck C, Butterworth CE Jr: Ascorbate-cholesterol-lecithin interactions: factors of potential importance in the pathogenesis of atherosclerosis. Am J Clin Nutr, 27:866–876, 1974

7. Harper HA: Précis de biochimie. (ed 4, French). Quebec, Les Presses de l'Université Laval, 1977

8. Clément G: Contribution à l'étude de l'absorption intestinale et de l'utilisation par l'organisme des acides gras à chaînes courtes et moyennes. In Les Corps Gras Alimentaires [Supplément au fascicule 2 des Cahiers de Nutrition et de Diététique IV:29–49]. Paris, Presses Universitaires de France, 1969

9. Snyder F (ed): Lipid metabolism in mammals, vol 1. New York, Plenum Press, 1977

10. Smyth DH (ed): Intestinal absorption: Biomembranes, vol 4B. London, Plenum Press, 1974

11. Finer EG, Henry R, Leslie RB, Robertson RN: NMR studies of pig low- and high-density serum lipoproteins. Molecular motions and morphology. Biochim Biophys Acta, 380:320–337, 1975

12. Marcheboeuf M: Recherches sur les phosphoaminolipides et les stérides du sérum et du plasma sanguins; entraînement des phospholipides, des stérols et des stérides par les diverses fractions au cours du fractionnement des protéines du sérum. Bull Soc Chim Biol, 11:268–293, 1929

13. Marcheboeuf M: Recherches sur les phosphoaminolipides et les stérides du sérum et du plasma sanguins; étude physico-chimique de la fraction protéidique la plus riche en phospholipides et en stérides. *Bull Soc Chim Biol*, 11:485–503, 1929

14. Gofman JW, Lindgren F, Elliott H, Mantz W, Hewitt J, Strisower B, Herring V: The role of lipids and lipoproteins in atherosclerosis. *Science*, 111:166–171, 1950

15. Fredrickson DS, Gordon RS Jr: Transport of fatty acids. *Physiol Rev*, 38:585–630, 1958

16. Fredrickson DS, Levy RI, Lees RS: Fat transport in lipoproteins—an integrated approach to mechanisms and disorders. *N Engl J Med*, 276:34–44, 1967

17. Fredrickson DS, Levy RI, Lees RS: Fat transport in lipoproteins—an integrated approach to mechanisms and disorders (continued). *N Engl J Med*, 276:94–103, 1967

18. Fredrickson DS, Levy RI, Lees RS: Fat transport in lipoproteins—an integrated approach to mechanisms and disorders (continued). *N Engl J Med*, 276:215–225, 1967

19. Fredrickson DS, Levy RI, Lees RS: Fat transport in lipoproteins—an integrated approach to mechanisms and disorders (concluded). *N Engl J Med*, 276:273–281, 1967

20. Jackson RL, Morrisett JD, Gotto AM Jr: Lipoprotein structure and metabolism. *Physiol Rev*, 56:259–316, 1976

21. Gotto AM Jr, Shepherd J, Scott LW, Manis E: Primary hyperlipoproteinemia and dietary management. In Levy R, Rifkind B, Dennis B, Ernst N (eds) *Nutrition, Lipids, and Coronary Heart Disease*, pp 247–283. New York, Raven Press, 1979

22. Morrisett JD, Jackson RL, Gotto AM Jr: Lipoproteins: structure and function. *Annu Rev Biochem*, 44:183–207, 1975

23. Goldstein JL, Brown MS: The low-density lipoprotein pathway and its relationship to atherosclerosis. *Annu Rev Biochem*, 46:897–930, 1977

24. Rodbell M: The removal and metabolism of chylomicrons by adipose tissue *in vitro*. *J Biol Chem*, 235:1613–1620, 1960

25. Smith LC, Pownall HJ, Gotto AM Jr: The plasma lipoproteins: structure and metabolism. *Annu Rev Biochem*, 47:751–777, 1978

26. Alaupovic P, Lee DM, McConathy WJ: Studies on the composition and structure of plasma lipoproteins. Distribution of lipoprotein families in major density classes of normal human plasma lipoproteins *Biochim Biophys Acta*, 260:689–707, 1972

27. Bergström S, Sjövell J: The isolation of prostaglandin. *Acta Chem Scand*, 11:1086, 1957

28. Samuelsson B, Paoletti R: In Samuelsson B, Paoletti R (eds) *Advances in prostaglandin and thromboxane research*, Vol 1 and 2. New York, Raven Press, 1976

29. Curtis-Prior PB: *Prostaglandins. An introduction to their biochemistry, physiology and pharmacology*. New York, North-Holland, 1976

30. Kolata GB: Thromboxanes: The power behind the prostaglandins? *Science*, 190:770–771, 812, 1975

2

The technology of edible fats and oils

INTRODUCTION

The consumption of fats by Canadians has remained practically constant since 1950, varying only by 6–10 per cent over the years and settling at about 25 kilograms per capita since 1970. The nature of the fats consumed, however, has changed (Fig 17). The consumption of butter, for example, fell by 50 per cent between 1950 and 1975, whereas that of margarine increased by 70 per cent and that of shortenings and shortening oils by 86 per cent[1].

Margarines and shortenings are the products of a technology based on chemical and physicochemical reactions which modify, sometimes extensively, the chemical composition of the parent fats and oils. The application of this technology introduces into the food chain some types of fatty acids entirely different from those found naturally in non-treated vegetable oils. These new types of fatty acids are positional and geometrical isomers of natural fatty acids (*see* Chapter 1). They have the same carbon-chain length and the same number of double bonds as the natural compounds. They become positional isomers when the double bonds are found at different places on the carbon chain and geometrical isomers when the molecule takes the *trans* configuration around the double bonds.

In some respects, both types of isomer should be considered as kinds of food additives and their safety more thoroughly established. Consumers, many nutritionists and probably physicians, in general, are not aware of the presence of these new substances now appearing in foods. In addition, the publicity surrounding margarines and shortenings has led us to believe that fats modified by chemical technology have the same characteristics of purity as the parent material. It would therefore seem helpful to give some basic information on the technology used in the production of mar-

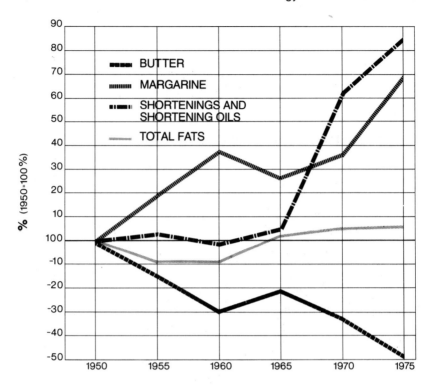

Fig. 17—*Trends in fat consumption in Canada (1950 = 100).*

(Based on Watts *et al*[1].)

The consumption of total fats by Canadians has remained practically constant since 1950. The nature of fats consumed, however,
changed. The consumption of butter, for example, fell by 50 per
cent between 1950 and 1975, whereas that of margarine increased
by 70 per cent and that of shortenings and shortening oils by 86
per cent.

garines and margarine-like products and to inform the reader about the
extraction, refining and hydrogenation processes applied to vegetable fats
and oils.

EXTRACTION AND PURIFICATION OF EDIBLE OILS

Vegetable oils offered to Canadian consumers are derived mainly from
soybean, canola (rapeseed), corn and sunflower seed. The preparation of

these for the extraction and purification of their oil consists of several steps such as trashing, decortication, grinding and flaking. These preliminary operations are essential for better contact with the solvent, thus ensuring better extraction.

Extraction

The industrial extraction of vegetable oils is usually achieved with hexane as solvent. Hexane is a hydrocarbon obtained from the distillation of petroleum. Its cost remains low compared with other organic solvents and it can be recovered *in toto* after extraction. Only traces of hexane, therefore, are found in crude oil after extraction. In certain cases and for certain seeds, the hydraulic press is still used; this technique of course requires no solvent.

However obtained, the extract (crude oil) is a mixture of fatty substances containing, in addition to the desired triglycerides, such substances as phospholipids, carotenoid and chlorophyll pigments, free fatty acids, tocopherols, phytosterols and minerals. The crude oil extracted from certain plants may also contain toxic substances such as isothiocyanates in the case of crude canola oil and aflatoxins, in the case of peanut oil where it is used. Isothiocyanates are substances which interfere with the normal activity of the thyroid gland and, as a result, cause goiter. Aflatoxins are toxins produced by molds growing on the peanuts and are extremely toxic to humans. The consumption of crude oils, therefore, is potentially dangerous.

Degumming

Degumming is ridding crude oil of a mixture of substances which in consistency and appearance resemble gums. These are phospholipids (for example, lecithins), true gums, protein-like compounds and complex polysaccharides. When heated at 60–90°C with water and phosphoric acid, they become hydrated, go into the aqueous phase and can then be removed by centrifugation. This operation also removes chlorophyll, calcium, magnesium and certain oligo-elements like iron and copper.

Refining

Refining is a process aimed primarily at lowering the amount of free fatty acids remaining in the oil after degumming. This is necessary in order to comply with standards advocated by agencies responsible for the wholesomeness of foods. Free fatty acids are undesirable because they indicate poor oil quality. When high quality oil is improperly stored, free fatty acids appear, caused by the hydrolysis of triglycerides.

Sodium hydroxide or a mixture of sodium hydroxide and sodium carbonate are the reagents most commonly used in refining edible oils. The oil and reagents are stirred for the appropriate time to allow the desired chemical reaction to take place, that is the production of soaps (sodium salts of fatty acids). The fatty acids in the form of soaps enter the aqueous phase, and are separated by centrifugation. In addition to fatty acids, this operation produces the soap stock which contains residual phospholipids, protein-like substances, pigments, calcium, magnesium and oligo-elements, amongst others.

Bleaching

In most cases refined edible oils are still highly colored, usually red or yellow; as a result they must undergo an additional process to eliminate this undesirable pigmentation and so obtain a product of reproducible color. The bleaching of vegetable oils is generally carried out with adsorbing substances such as Fuller's earth, activated charcoal or other adsorbant. The oil is brought into contact with these adsorbants for a period generally ranging from 15 to 30 minutes at temperatures of from 80 to 90°C or even 100°C. Usually, the activated clays have to be treated with sulphuric or hydrochloric acid to increase their adsorbing power.

During this process, the carotenoid pigments such as β-carotene and chlorophyll are retained on the adsorbing substance, while the oil is acquiring the color more commonly seen by the consumer. Decoloration also eliminates certain organic substances of the polycyclic and aromatic hydrocarbon families, when these are present in the refined oil.

Bleaching may be considered a drastic process as it leads to the formation of peroxides and conjugated fatty acids from polyunsaturated fatty acids. It is suspected that derivatives of phytosterols are formed during this process, the biological significance of which is still unknown[2].

In some cases, bleaching is carried out in vacuum at temperatures much higher than those mentioned above. This reduces the risk of peroxidation but causes the formation of positional and geometrical isomers of unsaturated fatty acids. The significance of these isomers in the diet will be discussed in a later section.

Deodorization

Even when refined and bleached, vegetable oils still retain their characteristic pungent odor and unpleasant taste. This is a serious handicap in products meant to imitate animal fats, particularly butter. Thus deodorization is essential to rid vegetable oils of the substances responsible for such undesirable odors and tastes.

As these substances are generally more volatile than triglycerides, they can be removed by high pressure steam distillation. In most cases the process requires temperatures of 240–270°C and holding times of 30–60 minutes. As the oil cools, it is customary to add citric acid as an antioxidant. When deodorization is well done, it is almost impossible to tell one vegetable oil from another, on the basis of odor and taste.

Apart from eliminating unpleasant substances to improve the taste and smell, deodorization will remove peroxides and residual fatty acids. It will also lower the phytosterol and tocopherol content. Thus deodorization tends to reduce substantially the vitamin E activity of the processed oil, as compared with the natural oil. But deodorization has the great advantage of removing pesticide residues and certain mycotoxins.

The high temperature at which deodorization is carried out causes the formation of many isomers of unsaturated fatty acids. In fact, the degree of isomerization is often indicative of the care with which the process has been carried out. Linear and cyclic dimers and polymers may also be formed, the biological activity of which is unknown. Deodorization is, therefore, a drastic process, and should be performed with care.

Some of the processes just described are also applied to fats of animal origin such as lard, edible tallow and fish oils. The conditions of extraction and refining, and of other processes, vary according to the nature of the material to be processed. However, the processes applied to animal products in general need not be as drastic and extensive as those applied to vegetable oils. This is because metabolically the host animal may not have absorbed toxic substances, phytosterols, undigestible substances or compounds responsible for strong odors and unpleasant taste. As a matter of fact, compared with vegetable fats, animal fats have already undergone several purification steps.

Nevertheless, it must be acknowledged that edible oil technology has made possible the preparation, from absolutely unedible vegetable products such as canola seeds, dietary fats which are highly digestible and which have excellent nutritional qualities. On the whole, it must be realized, however, that from the kernel on its golden ear to the *pure* corn oil (rather, purified corn oil), there is a whole world of technology which, in some cases, brings about changes in the oil which are still a cause of concern to biologists and nutritionists.

PARTIAL HYDROGENATION OF VEGETABLE OILS

The composition and the physical and chemical properties of shortenings and margarines largely depend on the degree of hydrogenation of the vegetable oils used as parent materials. Vegetable oils are naturally high in unsaturated fatty acids. Soybean oil, for example, contains approximately 80 per cent monounsaturated and polyunsaturated fatty acids, as compared to 33 per cent for butter and 55 per cent for lard[3]. This high degree of unsaturation means that natural soybean oil has a melting point which is too low and a degree of instability which is too high for it to be readily accepted by the food industry.

Partial hydrogenation reduces the degree of unsaturation of all vegetable oils and gives them physical and chemical properties which are well adapted to the needs of the food industry in general and to the baking industry in particular. Hence the partial hydrogenation of vegetable oils is one of the most important chemical processes used in the food industry. Basically, it consists of introducing hydrogen atoms at the points of unsaturation on the molecules of linolenic, linoleic and oleic acids present in the selected oils (Fig 18). These are the three major unsaturated fatty acids found in vegetable oils. The reaction takes place under pressure at a temperature of 120–210°C in the presence of hydrogen and a catalyst, generally nickel. Fig 18 shows the reaction in its simplest form. Many chemical reactions take place simultaneously so that the composition of the final product, depending on the conditions used, may vary considerably.

The following are among the changes resulting from partial hydrogenation of vegetable oils:

* The formation of saturated fatty acids; for example, oleic acid may yield stearic acid.
* The formation of *trans* isomers; for example, oleic acid may become elaidic acid (*trans*-C18:1), a *trans* monoene (*see* Fig 19), and linoleic acid may yield *trans* dienes (*trans, trans*-C18:2 or *cis, trans*-C18:2).
* The formation of positional isomers; for example, the double bond of oleic acid may move from carbon 9 (normal position for oleic acid) to carbon 8 or to carbons 10, 11 or 12 to yield *cis* positional isomers, or from carbon 9 to carbons 6, 8, 10, 11, 12, 13 or 14 to yield isomers of the *trans* series.
* The formation of conjugated fatty acids; in this case, the double bonds on the fatty acid molecule may take the following sequence: CH_3 ... $CH=CH.CH=$ ... $COOH$ for the conjugated and CH_3 ... $CH=CH.CH_2.CH=$ ... $COOH$ for the natural fatty acid.

As a result, the fatty acid composition of a partially hydrogenated vegetable oil retains little similarity to that of the parent or natural oil. The difference between the composition of the natural oil and that of the partially hydrogenated oil becomes greater as the degree of hydrogenation increases.

How then does the composition of partially hydrogenated oils generally compare with that of natural vegetable oils? Unfortunately, it is impossible,

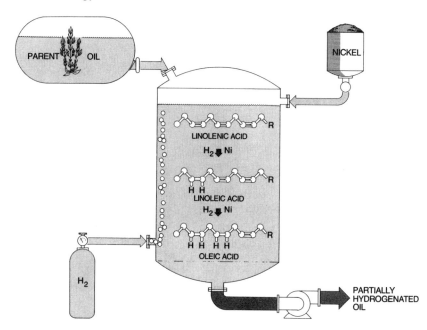

Fig. 18—*Illustration of the partial hydrogenation process applied to vegetable oils.*

The partial hydrogenation of vegetable oils is an industrial process by which unsaturated fatty acids are progressively saturated to produce an oil or a fat having physical and chemical properties different from those of the parent oil. The process is based on a chemical reaction in which hydrogen atoms are introduced into fatty acid molecules at the point of unsaturation to saturate the double bonds normally found in the natural vegetable oils. *Trans* fatty acids isomers are formed during the process.

at this stage, to answer the question satisfactorily. The identification and quantitative determination of the many isomers formed during the partial hydrogenation process represent tasks currently of little interest to chemists.

Nevertheless, it is possible from the little data available to conclude that after partial hydrogenation, the isomers of oleic acid (C18:1) are likely to be found in the ratios given in Fig 19. Among the *cis* isomers, nearly 75 per cent have their double bond on carbon 12. In the case of *trans* isomers, approximately 30 per cent have their double bond on carbon 10 while others may have their double bond on carbons 6, 7, 8—up to carbon 14. In the parent oil before hydrogenation, on the other hand, the C18:1 acid series is wholly accounted for by *cis* oleic acid.

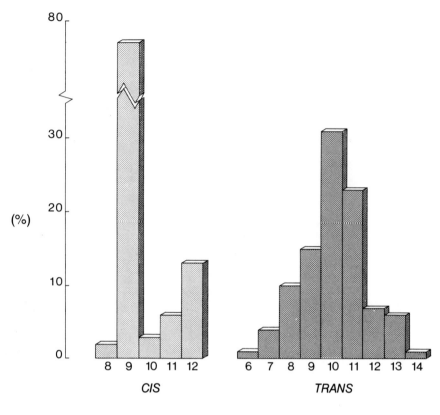

Fig. 19—Cis *and* trans *isomers of oleic acid (C*18:1*) found in a partially hydrogenated vegetable oil.*

(Adapted from data reported by Scholfield, Davison and Dutton[4], and by Dutton[5].)

Partial hydrogenation of vegetable oils leads to the formation of many isomers of the unsaturated fatty acids. The identification and quantitative measurement of these fatty acid isomers is difficult and tedious. The few data which are available show, however, that most *trans* isomers of oleic acid have their double bond on carbon 10 or 11, but a whole range of other isomers may have the double bond on one or the other of carbons 6 to carbon 14. *Cis* isomers are also found. The real nature and the exact quantities of the different *cis* and *trans* fatty acid isomers present in any partially hydrogenated vegetable oil remain unknown and unpredictable.

Thus, partially hydrogenated vegetable oil would contain a series of new molecules not found in the parent oil. Furthermore, it would be practically impossible to predict with accuracy either the nature or the content of these new molecules. As a result, between the parent vegetable oil, sometimes labeled *pure*, and the partially hydrogenated product, which is the starting material for many substitute animal fats, there is a world of chemistry that alters profoundly the composition and physicochemical properties of natural oils.

Partial hydrogenation of vegetable oils, however, is of great benefit in food technology. The degree of unsaturation being reduced, the stability of the hydrogenated product is greatly improved, and its tendency to oxidize is lessened. For example, soybean oil, which contains about 7 per cent linolenic acid[3], a three double bond fatty acid, is extremely sensitive to oxidation and peroxidation. Partial hydrogenation transforms the linolenic acid into a compound which is less unsaturated and, as a result, the processed soybean oil becomes much more stable than the parent oil.

Partial hydrogenation moreover hardens the oil by raising its melting point. In this regard, the production of *trans* isomers is desirable because their melting point is always higher than that of the natural *cis* fatty acids. Thus the melting point of oleic acid (*cis*-C18:1) is about 10°C, whereas it is 54°C for elaidic acid (*trans*-C18:1), its *trans* isomer. Similarly, the melting point of linoleic acid (*cis*-C18:2), which is −11°C, rises to 15°C when it becomes *trans*-C18:2. The isomers of unsaturated fatty acids, obtained through partial hydrogenation, are thus desirable in food technology because they help to harden the resulting fats and give them the plasticity and the melting points characteristic of butter or other animal fats which they are meant to imitate.

Indeed, partial hydrogenation of vegetable oils represents a major victory for food technology, but this process changes markedly the nature of the parent oil and introduces into the food chain, sometimes in large quantities, new types of molecules that some might classify as food additives. Dutton[6] wrote: "If the hydrogenation process were discovered today, it probably could not be adopted by the oil industry". And, he added, ". . . the basis for such comment lies in the recent awareness of our prior ignorance concerning the complexity of isomers formed during hydrogenation and their metabolic and physiological fate". As a matter of fact, the partial hydrogenation process adopted by the industry is still highly empirical and is guided much more by the characteristics of the product to be obtained than by any attempt to control the nature and the quantity of isomers generated.

Partially hydrogenated vegetable oils which are the basis for the production of substitutes for animal fats, have many properties which are still unknown to physicians, nutritionists, health professionals and other professionals interested in public health, and to the public in general. We shall attempt in the next chapter to summarize present knowledge on the metabolism of these little known molecules, the *trans* isomers.

REFERENCES

1. Watts TA, Gullett EA, Sabry JH, Liefeld JP: Tendances de la consommation alimentaire et de la nutrition au Canada. (Groupe de la politique alimentaire: Rapport). Ministère de la Consommation et des Corporations, Canada, Ottawa, October, 1977

2. FAO and WHO: F.A.O. Food and Nutrition paper 3: Dietary fats and oil in human nutrition: a joint F.A.O./W.H.O. report. Food and Agriculture Organization of the United Nations, Rome, 1977

3. Sheppard AJ, Iverson JL, Weihrauch JL: Composition of selected dietary fats, oils, margarines, and butter. In Kuksis A (ed) *Handbook of Lipid Research*, vol 1, Fatty Acids and Glycerides, pp 341–379. New York, Plenum Press, 1978

4. Scholfield CR, Davison VL, Dutton HJ: Analysis for geometrical and positional isomers of fatty acids in partially hydrogenated fats. *J Am Oil Chem Soc*, 44:648–651, 1967

5. Dutton HJ: Hydrogenation of fats and its significance. In Emken EA, Dutton HJ (eds) *Geometrical and Positional Fatty Acid Isomers*, pp 1–16. American Oil Chemists' Society, Monograph 6, Illinois, 1979

6. Dutton HJ: *Progress in the chemistry of fats and other lipids*, vol 9. Oxford, Pergamon Press, 1971

3

The enigma of the *trans* fatty acids

INTRODUCTION

Margarines and shortenings, man made equivalents of butter and lard, contain different amounts of partially hydrogenated vegetable oils. As described in the preceding chapter, the partial hydrogenation of vegetable oils, such as corn and soybean, modifies the chemical and physical properties of their fatty acids. Partial hydrogenation, for example, transforms some fatty acids into new compounds called fatty acid *isomers*. We have already distinguished between positional and geometrical isomers of unsaturated fatty acids in Chapter 1. Geometrical isomers are illustrated in Fig 3 in which it is seen that the *cis*-isomers are curved at the point of unsaturation, while the *trans*-isomers are linear. The natural vegetable oils contain only *cis*-isomers, while the partially hydrogenated oils contain variable amounts of *trans*-isomers.

All foods containing partially hydrogenated vegetable oils have some *trans*-isomers of unsaturated fatty acids. In some cases, these may constitute as much as 36 per cent of the total fatty acids (Table 6). The processing of vegetable oils therefore may introduce into our foods large amounts of new types of compounds which, in some respects, could be considered as food additives.

Both the scientific community and the edible fats and oils industry have made little comment on the introduction of these *trans* fatty acids into foodstuffs. Little research has been done on the fate of these particular *additives* in the human body or on their possible effects on health. The government authorities responsible for the regulations concerning processed foods have remained silent with regard to permissible levels, labeling and safety of *trans* fatty acids. Perhaps they had no choice in view of the lack of information on the subject.

It is difficult to understand why there has been little comment on this topic. Even the promotion of foods high in polyunsaturated fatty acids

TABLE 6

TRANS FATTY ACID CONTENT OF SOME FOODS
(percent of total fatty acids)*

Foods	*Total* trans fatty acids
Bread and rolls	10.4 to 27.9
Cakes	10.1 to 24.0
Crackers	2.8 to 31.6
French fries	4.6 to 35.1
Instant and canned puddings	30.5 to 36.1
Stick margarines	18.0 to 36.0
Soft margarines	11.2 to 21.3
Shortenings	13.0 to 37.3
Snack chips and pretzels	14.4 to 33.4
Butter	<0.1 to 1.2

* From Enig et al[1]

The *trans* fatty acids found in foods are mainly *trans* monoenes, but dienes and trienes are also present. The content of *trans* fatty acids is generally expressed as a percentage of total fatty acids. Since fatty acids represent 95 per cent of dietary fats and oils, there is close agreement between the *trans* fatty acid content expressed as a percentage of total fatty acids and the content expressed as a percentage of the given fat. This table shows the extent to which the content of *trans* fatty acids may vary, not only from one food to another, but also from one sample of a given food to another.

failed to acknowledge their existence; nor was much attention paid to their possible ill effects. From time to time some isolated reports[1-6] reminded the scientific community that margarines, shortenings and foods made with partially hydrogenated vegetable oils contained various quantities of *trans* fatty acids from these oils and that these isomers could possibly have adverse effects on health. In a recent report discussed later in this chapter, Professor Keeney and his colleagues of the University of Maryland indicated that there is a possible association between the consumption of *trans* fatty acids and certain types of cancer. Soon thereafter, the mass media, the consumers and several scientists began to ask questions concerning *trans* fatty acids, their presence in foods, their role in nutrition and their possible effects on health.

In Canada, the consumption of processed food products containing partially hydrogenated vegetable oils, potentially rich in *trans*-isomers, increased considerably during the last three decades (Fig 17). In that time, the annual consumption of margarines and shortenings, for example, increased from 7 to nearly 15 kg per capita[7]. If the trends shown in Fig 20 are indicative of the future consumption of margarines and shortenings, it is clear that the intake of *trans* fatty acids by Canadians and probably by North Americans in general will increase considerably. It is important therefore to know the actual quantities of *trans* fatty acids consumed by the general public and to examine the possible effect of these compounds on lipid metabolism. We shall attempt to summarize the available scientific information concerning *trans* fatty acids, hoping to resolve the uncertainties which still surround them and throw some light on their possible effects on health.

TRANS FATTY ACIDS IN MARGARINES

Two main types of margarines are available: "print" and "tub". Print margarines have a higher melting point than soft ones; tub margarines therefore have a better spreadability than hard ones even when kept in the refrigerator. Tub margarines are also believed to be higher in linoleic acid (C18:2ω6). Consequently tub margarines would be considered more desirable than print margarines as far as their content of polyunsaturated fatty acids is concerned.

Both types of margarine are made from mixtures of partially hydrogenated and unhydrogenated oils. The most commonly used vegetable oils for margarine manufactured in Canada are soybean, canola (rapeseed), corn and sunflower seed. A certain amount of animal fat and fish oils may also be incorporated into margarines. Margarines may be processed from single vegetable oils or from a mixture of oils, partially hydrogenated oils being most frequently used. Since it is not essential to declare on the label the quantities of the different fats and oils used in the preparation of margarines, the industry is free to choose mixtures formulated by a computer and based solely on the cost of the raw materials available on the market at any given time. Each batch of margarine could well be derived from a mixture chosen partly on the basis of the cost of the raw materials. This licence in the choice of raw materials as well as in their proportions could explain why so many brands of margarine, all chemically different but having similar physical characteristics such as texture, melting point or spreadability, have invaded the North American food market.

Under such conditions, one might rightly suspect that the *trans* fatty acid content of margarines as well as their chemical composition will vary considerably from one brand to another and even from one batch to another within the same brand. In fact, an examination of the composition of 150 samples[8-10] of different brands of margarines sold in Canada revealed that the *trans* fatty acid content ranged from 9.9 to 47.8 per cent for print margarines and from 4.4 to 43.3 per cent for tub margarines (Fig 20). The averages are 31 and 17 per cent for print and tub margarines, respectively. Because of this wide variation, brands of both the print and tub margarines may have the same *trans* fatty acid content. At the present time, margarines are labeled in such a way that no indication is given as to the content of *trans* fatty acids.

The content of *trans* monoenes (C18:1) and of *trans* dienes (C18:2) in margarines sold in Canada is also given in Fig 20. The *trans* monoene

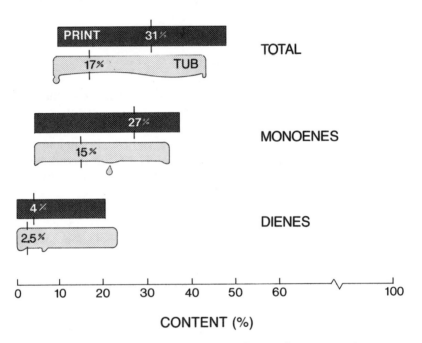

Fig. 20—Trans *fatty acid content of Canadian margarines.*
(Based on references [8-10].)

Canadian margarines in general are classified as print or tub margarines. On average, the print margarines contain 31 per cent *trans* fatty acids and the tub margarines 17 per cent. Variations between brands and within each type are considerable. Thus, the *trans* fatty acid content of any given sample may range from 10 to 40 per cent irrespective of type. The content of *trans* dienes is much lower than that of *trans* monoenes, but in both cases the variation from one sample to another is great. Consequently it is impossible to predict the content of *trans* fatty acids in any margarine based solely on the information appearing on the label.

content of print margarines averages 27 per cent as compared to 15 per cent for tub margarines. In both cases, the content of a given sample may be found within the range of 5–35 per cent. As for the *trans* dienes, the concentrations range from zero to approximately 20 per cent with an average of 4 per cent for print margarines and 2.5 per cent for tub margarines. As a result, it can only be stated with certainty that print margarines generally contain more *trans* fatty acids then tub margarines. For a given brand, however, it is impossible to predict with any assurance the *trans* fatty acid content based solely on the information given on the label.

In view of this situation, it appears necessary to assess the frequency with which a given concentration of *trans* fatty acids may be found in margarines presently sold, for example, in Canada. It is seen in Fig 21 that one third of Canadian margarines contain 10–20 per cent total *trans* fatty acids and approximately one quarter of them contain more than 30 per cent. In other words, if margarines were to be selected at random, one out of four would contain more than 30 per cent *trans* fatty acids, and one out

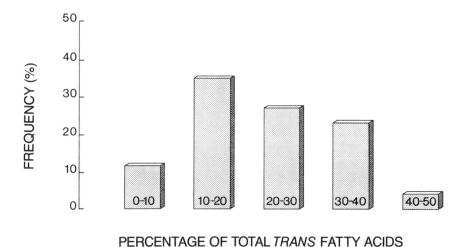

PERCENTAGE OF TOTAL *TRANS* FATTY ACIDS

Fig. 21—Frequency distribution of trans *fatty acids in margarines.*
(Based on references[9,10].)

This histogram shows that one third of margarines contain 10–20 per cent *trans* fatty acids and approximately one quarter of them contain more than 30 per cent. If margarines were to be selected at random, one out of two would contain more that 20 per cent *trans* fatty acids and one out of four, more than 30 per cent. Thus, margarines currently available contain large quantities of *trans* fatty acids.

of two, more than 20 per cent. Thus, margarines currently available contain large quantities of *trans* fatty acids.

TRANS FATTY ACIDS IN ANIMAL FATS

Feedstuffs used in the rations of farm animals contain on average 3–6 per cent fat, generally high in polyunsaturated fatty acids*. Yet butter fat and animal fats, in general, are low in polyunsaturated fatty acids. This is due to two important biological phenomena:

1. The biosynthesis of fatty acids in the animal body always yields saturated and monounsaturated* fatty acids.
2. The partial biohydrogenation of fatty acids taking place in the rumen of cattle or other ruminants also yields saturated and monounsaturated fatty acids.

Let us consider the second phenomenon since it is also responsible for the production of small amounts of *trans* fatty acids which are found in some animal fats. The biohydrogenation of polyunsaturated fatty acids takes place in the rumen of animals providing milk and meat to man: cattle, sheep and goats.

The rumen is a large compartment in the digestive tract of these animals with a capacity of 130–270 liters in cattle. An extensive microbial fermentation takes place therein and the fibrous part of the feed is digested. As a consequence, vegetable material high in cellulose and unfit for human consumption is degraded and fermented to yield small fatty acid molecules such as acetic acid ($C2:0$), propionic acid ($C3:0$) and butyric acid ($C4:0$). These small molecules are absorbed into the blood and are used as sources of energy or as raw material for the biosynthesis of milk, butterfat and meat.

The composition of the rumen microflora and the reactions associated with its activity are still a mystery to microbiologists, although a great deal of research has been carried out on the subject. The phenomenon of biohydrogenation associated with the activity of the rumen microflora is, however, well understood[11]. Linoleic ($C18:2$) and linolenic acids ($C18:3$) taken as grass, hay or other vegetable product by ruminants are hydrogenated in the rumen and transformed into saturated fatty acids, for example, stearic acid ($C18:0$). This process is governed by complex enzyme systems which are unique to the rumen microflora[11].

The efficacy of the rumen microflora in hydrogenating these unsaturated fatty acids is shown in Fig 22. It can be seen, for example, that the sum of unsaturated fatty acids equivalent to 60 per cent of fatty acids in

---

* See Chapter 1.

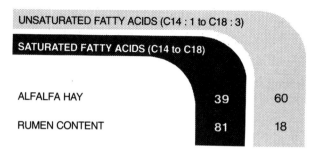

Fig. 22—Fatty acid composition of lipids extracted from alfalfa hay compared to that of lipids extracted from the rumen content (values expressed as per cent of total fatty acids in the lipid extract).

(Data published by Katz and Keeney[12].)

In cattle and all other ruminants, the symbiotic microflora of the rumen partially hydrogenates the polyunsaturated fatty acids ingested in feed. Consequently, the highly unsaturated fat ingested via alfalfa hay is transformed into saturated fat in the rumen. This phenomenon explains why it is impossible to modify the polyunsaturated fatty acid composition of milk fat and depot fat in ruminants by changing the fat in the ration. The biohydrogenation process that takes place in the rumen is regulated by an unchanging and unchangeable biological system. As a result, the low *trans* fatty acid content of butterfat and tallow is practically invariable.

---

alfalfa hay drops to 18 per cent in the rumen; on the other hand, the sum of saturated fatty acids is increased from 39 in alfalfa hay to 81 per cent in the rumen. This phenomenon explains, at least in part, why butter fat and tallow are always high in saturated fatty acids, although the feedstuffs consumed by cattle contain large proportions of polyunsaturated fatty acids.

The enzymes of the rumen microflora responsible for the biohydrogenation include isomerases. These enzymes can produce a certain number of *trans* fatty acids, for example vaccenic acid, one of the most important fatty acids so produced. It has a chain length of 18 carbon atoms with one double bond on carbon 11 from the carboxyl group; it is a geometrical and positional isomer of oleic acid (*cis*-$C18:1\Delta^9$) and its formula is *trans*-$C18:1\Delta^{11}$*.

---

* *See Table 1.*

Vaccenic acid represents 75 per cent of the *trans* isomers of oleic acid in the rumen content[12]. *Trans* dienes and trienes are found only in traces in the rumen content. Vaccenic acid, like other isomers formed by bio-hydrogenation in the rumen, may be absorbed by the intestine, circulated in the blood, and is ultimately found in meat and milk fat.

It is important to note that the biohydrogenation process as described here takes place under conditions of uniform temperature, humidity and pressure. It is regulated by an almost unvarying biological system. As a result, the low *trans* fatty acid content of butterfat and ruminant body fat is practically invariable.

The low content of *trans* fatty acids in butter and beef fat has been known for some time. Data published prior to 1970, however, should be interpreted with caution because the analytical techniques then available were not wholly satisfactory. These improved considerably during the following decade. According to most recent data, the *trans* fatty acid content of butter is probably less than 2.5 per cent[1,13-15].

A few studies indicated some differences between summer and winter butter with regard to *trans* fatty acid content. During the summer, when animals are on pasture, it may double. This has been observed in France and in the United Kingdom[15,16]. In both cases, vaccenic acid (*trans*-$C18:1\Delta^{11}$) represented 60 per cent of the positional and geometrical isomers of oleic acid[17]. Apart from this possible seasonal variation, which has not been studied in Canada and North America in general, it may be assumed that the *trans* fatty acid content of milk fat and butter, is, for all practical purposes, less than 2 per cent and probably remains constant throughout the year. It should also be noted, as far as milk is concerned, that regardless of the trade mark or the time of year, the *trans* fatty acid content remains low.

The *trans* fatty acid content of beef and lamb fat is practically unknown. It is possible however, that *trans* fatty acids in tallow are less than 0.5 per cent[14]. As a result, the intake of *trans* fatty acids via meat is minimal, if not negligeable.

Lastly, in our day-to-day life, less than 5 per cent of total *trans* fatty acids consumed is supplied by animal fats; partially hydrogenated vegetable oils used in the preparation of numerous foods on the other hand supply more than 95 per cent[18].

INTAKE OF *TRANS* FATTY ACIDS

Estimating the daily intake of a given food is difficult, because the basic detailed data concerning the food habits of, for example, the Canadian population are not available. Attempting to calculate the daily intake of *trans* fatty acids meets with the same difficulties. Only approximate values can be calculated.

Enig in the United States of America and Renner in Canada have evaluated the intakes of *trans* fatty acids in their respective countries. Enig based her calculations partly on analyses of *trans* fatty acids carried out in her own laboratory and partly on the food consumption data published in Rizek, Friend and Page[19]. Renner based her calculations on food consumption trends and on average values for *trans* fatty acids in some food items.

According to Enig, the average intake of *trans* fatty acids in the United States is about 12 g per capita per day[18,20]; of this quantity, 4.8 per cent comes from animal fat and 95.2 per cent from partially hydrogenated vegetable oils used in many food items. In this case, *trans* fatty acids represent 8 per cent of the total fat in the diet. Renner calculated a value of 7.1g per capita per day but she used only margarines and shortenings as sources of *trans* fatty acids in the diet.

If adjustments are made to Renner's estimates in the light of the most recent data which includes foods other than margarines and shortenings[1,7] (Figs 20 and 21), the daily intake of *trans* fatty acids in Canada would be about 9.6 g per capita per day, with a possible maximum of 17.53 g (Table 7). Partially hydrogenated oils, in this case, would supply 94 per cent of total intake. For all practical purposes the amended data of Renner and those of Enig agree closely.

Average values calculated in this manner do not tell what the real intake is for a given individual or group of individuals in a given age group. Let us assume the case of a man, aged 20–39 years, whose diet is similar to that reported in Nutrition Canada[21] for that particular age group. The daily *trans* fatty acid intake for that individual will be 11.07 g on average with a maximum value of 17.05 g. Thus it is possible for the intake of *trans*

TABLE 7

INTAKE OF *TRANS* FATTY ACIDS IN CANADA

Sources	Fat[1] intake (g per day)	Trans *fatty acids*			
		Concentration (%)		Intake (g per day)	
		Average	Maximum	Average	Maximum
Butter	12.3	1.8	4.0	0.22	0.49
Milk	11.8	1.8	4.0	0.22	0.47
Margarine	15.5	22.4[2]	47.8	3.49	7.41
Shortening and shortening oil	23.0	20.0[3]	37.3	4.60	8.58
Salad oil	10.0	4.5	4.6	0.45	0.46
Meat (beef)	23.5	0.5	0.5	0.12	0.12
Total				9.10	17.53

[1] *Based on Watts et al*[7]
[2] *Based on* Figs 21 and 23
[3] *Based on Enig et al*[1]

fatty acids to be 12 g per day for the active class of the population in Canada; in that case the intake will be identical to that reported for the United States of America[20,22].

If the food consumption trends illustrated in Fig 17 hold true, it might be predicted that within a short time the intake of *trans* fatty acids in North America will represent more than 10 per cent of the total fat in the diet for a good part of the population.

METABOLISM OF *TRANS* FATTY ACIDS

The introduction of increasing amounts of *trans* fatty acids into our foods has attracted the attention of a few investigators. Some studies dealt with different aspects of the metabolism of these isomers including their digestibility, absorption, accumulation in the tissues, catabolism and incorporation into different membranes.

Elaidic acid (*trans*-C18:1Δ^9)—a *trans*-isomer of oleic acid—was the most frequently studied. It represents 15 per cent (Fig 19) of *trans* fatty acids found in partially hydrogenated vegetable oils. Unfortunately, the *cis* positional isomers of oleic acid as well as other positional or geometrical isomers of both dienes and monoenes, also found in partially hydrogenated vegetable oils, have not been investigated to the same degree as elaidic acid. Therefore the data available to date can only give a partial answer to the many questions raised concerning the metabolism of *trans* acids in our diet.

Digestibility and absorption

Dietary fats and oils consist of mixed triglycerides in which the fatty acids esterified with glycerol may be different for each of the three positions on the glycerol molecule (*see* Chapter 1). It is known that mixed triglycerides are normally well digested and well absorbed provided that reasonable quantities are ingested. Partially hydrogenated vegetable oils, incorporated into margarines, shortenings or other foods, are also mixed triglycerides. In view of the relatively high proportion of *trans* fatty acids formed during the partial hydrogenation process, the question may be raised as to what degree they may affect the digestibility and absorption of partially hydrogenated fats. Studies conducted with regard to this question show that elaidic acid (*trans*-C18:1Δ^9) appears in the lymph at the same rate as oleic (*cis*-C18:1Δ^9), stearic (C18:0) and palmitic (C16:0) acids[23] after being ingested in the form of triglycerides. The same is true also for the *trans* dienes which are absorbed at the same rate as linoleic acid (*cis, cis*-C18:2$\Delta^{9,12}$)[24]. It can be concluded that the *trans* fatty acids most commonly found in partially hydrogenated vegetable oils are digested and absorbed as well as their *cis* isomers which occur naturally in the parent oils before partial hydrogenation.

Trans fatty acids as sources of cellular energy

As we have just seen, *trans* fatty acids are absorbed and enter into the general blood circulation via the lymph in a manner similar to their *cis* isomers. Once they are introduced into the bloodstream, the *trans* fatty acids are transported to all body cells where they become available for many metabolic functions: they may be used as a source of energy, they may be deposited for future use and so forth. Here again, the question may be raised as to whether the *trans* fatty acids are recognized by the cellular enzyme systems so as to be metabolized differently from their *cis* isomers? Let us first study them as sources of energy.

A fatty acid molecule becomes a source of cellular energy through a series of reactions giving rise to the production of acetyl groups (CH_3COO^-), appearing in the form of acetyl CoA. A fatty acid having an 18 carbon chain will yield 9 acetyl CoA groups. These groups are oxidized via the Krebs cycle to yield carbon dioxide, water and energy in the form of high energy phosphate bonds (ATP)[25]. The series of reactions giving rise to the formation of acetyl CoA groups is known as β-oxidation. It is based on the activity of highly specialized enzyme systems. The question is raised as to whether these specific enzyme systems can distinguish between the *trans* fatty acids and their *cis*-isomers and, if so, to what extent is their activity affected?

The first experiments used fatty acids labeled with radioactive carbon. The results suggested that the rapidity with which the rat could oxidize fatty acids was about the same for elaidic (*trans*-C18:1Δ^9), oleic (*cis*-C18:1Δ^9) and palmitic (C16:0) acids. In fact, the amount of radioactive carbon dioxide produced after 50 hours was about the same for the three fatty acids. It was concluded that elaidic acid could be used as a source of cellular energy as effectively as its *cis*-isomer, oleic acid[22,26]. In these studies, however, the radioactivity was fixed exclusively to the carbon atom of the carboxyl group, so that the speed of reaction applied to the decarboxylation process rather than to β-oxidation as a whole.

On the other hand, applying similar technique, it was noted that *trans* dienes were metabolized more rapidly than their *cis*-isomers. In an attempt to explain this difference in the rate of oxidation, it was suggested that the *trans*-dienes are used exclusively as a source of energy whereas a certain proportion of the *cis*-isomer, linoleic acid, is retained in the body as an essential fatty acid[23,26,27]. It is possible, therefore, that the two types of isomer can be distinguished by the cellular enzyme systems. This subject will be taken up again later in this chapter.

In experiments using radioactive labels, the rate at which carbon dioxide (CO_2) is produced gives no indication as to the different oxidative pathways followed. It is well established, however, that *trans* dienes are oxidized by the liver mitochondria via the β-oxidation pathway. Furthermore, the oxidation is complete and leaves no residues of unsaturated short-chain molecules[27]. From present knowledge this would apply only to the *trans*-isomers of linoleic acid.

With regard to the isomers of oleic acid (*cis*-C18:1Δ⁹) there seem to be different metabolic uses for the *cis* and *trans* isomers. For example, cardiac muscle behaves differently depending on whether it is using oleic acid or its *trans* isomer, elaidic acid[28], as a source of energy. Furthermore, when these two isomers (*cis*- and *trans*-C18:1Δ⁹) are given to animals, 30 per cent of the *trans* isomer remains in the body as compared to 22 per cent of the *cis* isomer[29]. It is becoming evident that the *trans* isomers of the C18:1 acids are not metabolized in the same way as their *cis* isomers.

It was mentioned above that vaccenic acid (*trans*-C18:1Δ⁹), a geometrical and positional isomer of oleic acid (*cis*-C18:1Δ⁹) represents the major proportion of *trans* fatty acids found in milk fat and in ruminant fat (beef). The interest raised by the increasing content of *trans* fatty acids in our diet prompted some investigators at the University of Illinois to study some *trans* fatty acids of the C18:1 series with regard to their metabolism in mitochondria isolated from cardiac muscle[30]. Their results are summarized in Fig 23 and show:

(1) that the rate of metabolism via the β-oxidization pathway is faster for the *cis* than for the *trans* isomers; and

(2) that the rate of metabolism increases as the double bond moves away from the carboxyl group, for example C18:1Δ⁶ as compared to C18:1Δ¹¹.

As a consequence, the rate at which vaccenic acid, a *trans* isomer produced by biohydrogenation, is catabolized at the cellular level is closer to that of oleic acid, a natural *cis* isomer, than to that of elaidic acid, a *trans* isomer produced by partial hydrogenation of vegetable oils. As a result, vaccenic acid has less tendency to accumulate in the cardiac muscle than has elaidic acid. This property may have practical consequences as will be discussed later in this chapter.

The reason why *trans* isomers, particularly elaidic acid (*trans*-C18:1Δ⁹), are catabolized less rapidly than the *cis* isomers has been the subject of some investigations. At the cellular level, the catabolism of fatty acids takes place in a stepwise fashion as is illustrated in Fig 23. As mentioned earlier, specific enzyme systems are involved to produce one acetyl CoA group at each step. It was suspected that some enzyme within these systems might be able to recognize the *trans* double bonds and as a consequence be less efficient.

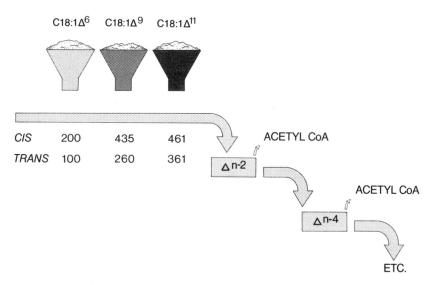

Fig. 23—*Relative rate of catabolism of geometrical and positional isomers of oleic acid* (cis-C18:1Δ^9). *(Rate for* trans-C18:1Δ^6 = 100*)*.

(Adapted from Lawson and Kummerow[30].)

Fatty acids used by the body as sources of energy are degraded through a series of reactions governed by specific and highly specialized enzymes. Fatty acids are progressively split into acetyl CoA groups according to the β-oxidation pathway and are ultimately oxidized via the Krebs cycle. The *cis* isomers are oxidized more rapidly than the *trans* and the rate of catabolism increases as the double bond moves away from the carboxyl group, for example C18:1Δ^6 as compared to C18:1Δ^{11}.

One enzyme involved in the dehydrogenation of fatty acids, a preliminary step in the formation of acetyl CoA groups, was the first one to be investigated. It was found (Fig 24) that the rate of dehydrogenation is faster for the *trans* than for the *cis* isomers. In all cases, the presence of a *trans* instead of a *cis* double bond in the carbon chain resulted in a stimulated activity of the enzyme acyl CoA dehydrogenase. Accordingly, the slower rate of catabolism of elaidic acid (*trans*-C18:1Δ^9), when compared to oleic acid (*cis*- C18:1Δ^9), could not be explained by an inhibition of this enzyme. Therefore, the explanation as to why *trans* fatty acids are used less rapidly than their *cis* isomers as sources of cellular energy must be sought elsewhere. Nevertheless, one fact remains: the *trans* fatty acids appearing in partially hydrogenated vegetable oils are recognized by the cellular enzymes and their activity is affected by the presence of these isomers.

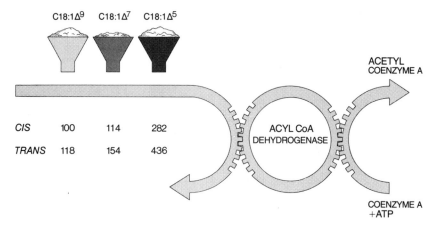

Fig. 24—*Relative rate of dehydrogenation of fatty acid isomers.*
(Rate for oleic acid = 100.)

(Adapted from references[31,32].)

The activity of the enzyme acyl-CoA dehydrogenase—an enzyme involved in the formation of acetyl CoA groups—is higher with the *trans* than with the *cis* isomers. The activity is slower as the double bond on the carbon chain moves away from the carboxyl group, for example $C18:1\Delta^5$ as compared to $C18:1\Delta^9$. The behavior of this particular enzyme with geometrical isomers, could not therefore explain the reduced rate of catabolism of the *trans* as compared to the *cis* fatty acid isomers when used for cellular energy.

In general, fatty acids are good sources of energy for cardiac muscle. Sometimes, 60–90 per cent of the energy metabolism of that organ may be explained by the oxidation of fatty acids. In this regard, let us recall that the *trans* fatty acid content of the diet has an influence on the *trans* fatty acid content of cellular lipids. For example, the elaidic acid (*trans*-$C18:1\Delta^9$) content of phospholipids* in mitochondria isolated from cardiac muscle increased from zero to over 23 per cent when monogastric animals were fed a diet based on a partially hydrogenated vegetable oil as compared to a diet based on the natural non-hydrogenated oil[33]. In view of this, is it not logical to think that the intake of *trans* fatty acids may eventually affect the normal metabolism of cardiac muscle?

In fact, some experiments have shown that phospholipids high in elaidic acid (*trans*-$C18:1\Delta^9$) were catabolized at a rate 200% slower than

---

* See Chapter 1.

oleic acid (*cis*-C18:1Δ^9).[31,32] In an attempt to explain this phenomenon, which is in agreement with observations made previously concerning the comparative rates of metabolism of *trans* and *cis* isomers, one of the enzymes involved in the formation of oleyl CoA and elaidoyl CoA from phospholipids present in cardiac muscle was examined. The comparative activity of this enzyme with the *cis* and *trans* isomers of the fatty acid C18:1Δ^9 failed to explain the discrimination made by the mitochondria of cardiac muscle between *cis* and *trans* fatty acids. It was then assumed that the limiting factor was not the activity of the enzyme systems involved in the cellular catabolism of fatty acids, but rather the speed with which the *trans* fatty acids, as compared to the *cis* isomers, are carried across the mitochondrial membranes.[31] Additional data are necessary, however, to confirm this hypothesis. Whatever the biochemical explanation, one fact remains: oleic acid (*cis*-C18:1Δ^9) is used more effectively as a source of cellular energy than its *trans* isomer, elaidic acid (*trans*-C18:1Δ^9). This is especially true for cardiac muscle.

The need for fatty acids to be used as sources of energy is increased considerably under severe stress.[32] For example, during a heart attack, the pulse rate may rise 3–4 times above normal. Under such conditions, the demand for energy is extreme and fatty acids must supply the major part of that energy. It is becoming difficult to rule out the possibility that the presence of *trans* fatty acids rather than the *cis* isomers, at the points of increased demand for energy due to stress, might be a limiting factor with serious consequences. As suggested by Kummerow[32] this possibility should be investigated further.

Trans fatty acids, phospholipids and cholesterol esters

Phospholipids and cholesterol esters (described in Chapter 1) play important roles in numerous biochemical and physiological body functions. It is known that the physicochemical properties of these compounds are markedly influenced by the nature of their component fatty acids and by the proportions in which these fatty acids are found. Many studies have shown that the fatty acid composition of the diet has a profound influence on both the nature and the proportions of the various fatty acids incorporated into the phospholipids and the cholesterol esters (Table 8). A diet high in *trans* fatty acids will reduce the proportion of oleic acid (*cis*-C18:1Δ^9) and increase the proportions of polyunsaturated and *trans* fatty acids in both the phospholipids and cholesterol esters. One explanation for this may be found in the fact that *trans* fatty acids behave as saturated rather than as unsaturated fatty acids with enzyme systems.

It is difficult to predict, in practical terms, what the effects of this phenomenon will be on the normal functioning of the body. For example, it is known that the enzymes involved in the synthesis of phospholipids

TABLE 8

INFLUENCE OF A DIET HIGH IN *TRANS* FATTY ACIDS ON THE FATTY ACID COMPOSITION OF BLOOD PHOSPHOLIPIDS AND CHOLESTEROL ESTERS
(per cent of total fatty acids)*

Fatty acid	Diet high in cis-C18:1	Diet high in trans-C18:1
PHOSPHOLIPIDS COMPOSITION		
Total saturated	50	42
Oleic (*cis*-C18:1)	32	16
Elaidic (*trans*-C18:1)	0.7	10
Linoleic (C18:2)	13	27
Linolenic (C18:3)	0.8	1.4
CHOLESTEROL ESTERS COMPOSITION		
Total saturated	22	21
Oleic (*cis*-C18:1)	38	20
Elaidic (*trans*-C18:1)	1.1	6
Linoleic (C18:2)	34	42
Linolenic (C18:3)	0.8	6.4

* Data taken from Schrock and Connor[34]

The fatty acid composition of the diet has an influence on the fatty acid composition of the lipid fractions in the body. Thus the presence of *trans* fatty acids in dietary fat has a profound influence on the fatty acid composition of phospholipids and cholesterol esters. This table shows that the intake of *trans* fatty acids greatly modifies both the nature and the proportions of fatty acids incorporated in blood phospholipids and cholesterol esters. It is seen that following the intake of *trans*-isomers, the *trans* and the polyunsaturated fatty acid content increases markedly while the saturated fatty acid and oleic acid content decreases. The practical significance of this phenomenon is still unknown.

---

tend to incorporate the saturated fatty acids at the α position of the phosphoglycerides, whereas the unsaturated fatty acids are incorporated at the β position. the *trans* unsaturated fatty acids are preferably incorporated as the α position as if they were saturated fatty acids, while their *cis* isomers are naturally incorporated at the β position (Fig 25). This reaction is the same for both the *trans* dienes and *trans* monoenes when a comparison is made with the respective *cis* isomers. The result is that both saturated and *trans* unsaturated fatty acids are incorporated in the α position leaving more opportunity for the *cis* polyunsaturated fatty acids to occupy the

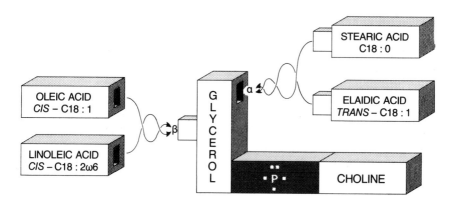

Fig. 25—Incorporation of trans *fatty acids and saturated fatty acids at the α position of phosphoglycerides.*

(Adapted from Lands *et al*[35].)

Cis monounsaturated fatty acids such as oleic acid (*cis*-C18:1) are preferentially incorporated at the β position of phospholipids, saturated fatty acids such as stearic acid (C18:0) preferentially at the α position. *Trans* monounsaturated fatty acids, such as elaidic acid (*trans*-C18:1), in this respect, are treated like saturated fatty acids and are incorporated at the α position rather than the β position as are the natural monounsaturated fatty acids. This results in a modification of the usual fatty acid composition of phospholipids.

β position. Consequently the phospholipids synthesized following a high intake of *trans* fatty acids would be unsaturated to a greater degree than if the natural *cis* isomers were consumed.[34]

Thus it is becoming evident that the enzymes involved in the distribution of fatty acids on the phospholipid molecules can distinguish between *trans* and *cis* fatty acids. In this respect, the *trans* fatty acids are treated like saturated rather than unsaturated fatty acids.

The enzymes involved in the hydrolysis of cholesterol esters can also distinguish between the geometrical isomers of fatty acids. Cholesterol esters with one molecule of a *trans* fatty acid, like elaidic acid (*trans*-C18:1Δ^9), for example, are hydrolyzed less rapidly than when the fatty acid is the natural *cis* isomer, oleic acid (*cis*-C18:1Δ^9). Here again, *trans* fatty acids are treated like saturated rather than unsaturated fatty acids[36]. It may be concluded that the *trans* fatty acids in some aspects of their metabolism could be regarded as saturated rather than as unsaturated fatty acids.

TRANS FATTY ACID DEPOSITS IN THE BODY

The type of fat taken in the diet has an influence on the composition of depot fats in man as in all non-ruminant animals. When unsaturated fats are consumed, the adipose tissue will have a high content of unsaturated fatty acids. All lipid fractions in the body will reflect to some extent the composition of the fat consumed. The relationship between this phenomenon and health is yet to be defined, but many questions in this connection are appropriate. The one raised here concerns the fate of dietary *trans* fatty acids in the human body.

First let us note that the very nature of dietary fats may influence the net amount of fat deposited in certain tissues. In the rat, for example, it has been shown that the intake of partially hydrogenated vegetable oil induced a greater accumulation of total lipids in the cardiac muscle than when milk fat or unprocessed vegetable oils was added to the diet (Fig 26). It has been shown also that feeding a partially hydrogenated oil may lower the VLDL in blood plasma while increasing the LDL, and not affect the HDL when compared to the feeding of the unprocessed oils. Similarly the fatty acid composition of the dietary fat may modify the fatty acid composition of all lipid fractions in the body. For example, following the intake of partially hydrogenated vegetable oil as compared to the unprocessed oil (Fig 27), the elaidic acid (*trans*-C18:1Δ^9) content of phospholipids isolated from cardiac muscle mitochondria increased from 0 to 23 per cent while the essential fatty acid content (linoleic acid C18:2 and arachidonic acid C20:4) dropped from 48 to 25 per cent.

Trans fatty acids accumulated not only in the phospholipids of the cardiac muscle mitochondria, but also in the adipose tissues and all lipid fractions in the entire body. Table 9 gives the maximum concentrations which have been observed in various tissues, organs or lipid fractions. In certain cases, the concentration may be 30–40 per cent of total fatty acids. In such cases, the experimental animals received large amounts of partially hydrogenated vegetable oils. What would be the respective concentrations if the animal had received for long periods amounts of partially hydrogenated oils comparable to those actually consumed in the diet? This question is still unanswered. Nevertheless it can be anticipated that a certain equilibrium will be reached between the concentration of *trans* fatty acid in the diet and that of the adipose tissues and the various lipid fractions in the body. Yet an important question remains concerning the effect of age and the period of time it would take to reach the concentration at which an equilibrium is attained.

While the practical consequences on health of the presence of *trans* fatty acids in various concentrations in the tissues are not yet known, one fact remains: the nature of dietary fats and the intake of *trans* fatty acids have a marked influence on both the quantity of fat deposited in tissues

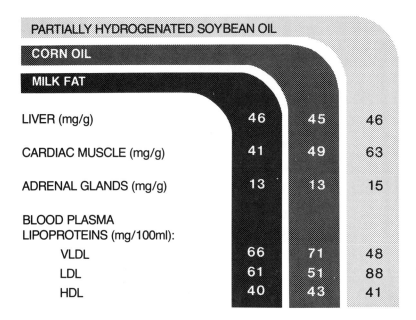

Fig. 26—*Effects of three types of dietary fat on the total lipid content of some tissues and on blood plasma lipoproteins in rat (mg/g of fresh tissue).*

(Data selected from Egwim and Kummerow[37].)

The type of fat consumed influences the amount of fat deposited in certain organs and tissues as well as the lipoprotein content of blood plasma. The intake of a partially hydrogenated vegetable oil when compared to milk fat influences markedly the amount of fat deposited in cardiac muscle; it also increases plasma LDL.

as well as the specific fatty acid and *trans* fatty acid composition of all lipid fractions in the body.

Trans fatty acids deposited in the fetus

The amount of *trans* fatty acid deposited in the fetuses of experimental animals is about 3 per cent of total fatty acids, even if the diet of the pregnant mother contained significant amounts of partially hydrogenated oils. It appears unlikely therefore that *trans* fatty acids accumulate to any great degree in the human fetus. It is not known whether the placenta serves as a barrier to *trans* fatty acids or whether the fetus metabolizes them more rapidly and more efficiently than the mother; whether the *trans*

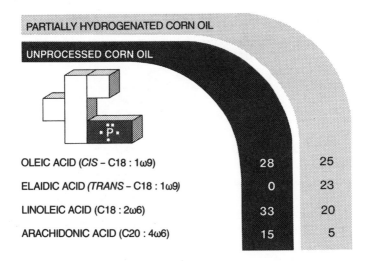

	PARTIALLY HYDROGENATED CORN OIL	UNPROCESSED CORN OIL
OLEIC ACID (*CIS* – C18 : 1ω9)	28	25
ELAIDIC ACID *(TRANS* – C18 : 1ω9)	0	23
LINOLEIC ACID (C18 : 2ω6)	33	20
ARACHIDONIC ACID (C20 : 4ω6)	15	5

Fig. 27—Effect of a diet containing partially hydro-genated corn oil on the fatty acid composition of phos-pholipids isolated from cardiac muscle (expressed as per cent of total fatty acids).

Data selected from Hsu and Kummerow[33].)

The fatty acid composition of phospholipids is greatly influenced by the intake of partially hydrogenated corn oil as compared to the unprocessed oil. The *trans* fatty acid content increases from 0 to 23 per cent when the partially hydrogenated oil is consumed compared to the unprocessed. On the other hand, the essential fatty acid content drops from 48 to 25 per cent. The consequences of this phenomenon on health are still a matter of speculation.

---

fatty acids accumulate in specific tissues or whether they are distributed uniformly in all parts of the fetus.

Transfer of *trans* fatty acids to milk

Trans fatty acids circulating in the blood pass through the barrier of the mammary gland and appear in milk. Human milk fat can contain 2–18 per cent of total fatty acids in the form of *trans* fatty acids.[42] It is likely that the consumption of partially hydrogenated vegetable oils in margarines and shortenings can account for these quantities.

The content of *trans* fatty acids in milk is influenced by the content in adipose tissues or in the diet or both. More research, however, is needed before it becomes possible to define quantitatively the relationship between the intake of *trans* fatty acids and their content in human milk.

TABLE 9

THE *TRANS* FATTY ACID CONTENT OF BODY LIPIDS FOLLOWING INTAKE OF PARTIALLY HYDROGENATED OILS (maximum values observed and expressed in terms of elaidic acid [*trans*-C18:1Δ^9] as per cent of total fatty acids)

Source of lipids	Trans fatty acids
Blood plasma[34,38]	
Total lipids	18
Triglycerides	15
Cholesterol esters	16
Phospholipids	23
Lipoproteins	
Cholesterol esters	16
Triglycerides	40
Phospholipids	23
Free fatty acids	23
Liver[6,39]	
Cholesterol esters	22–34
Phospholipids	16–22
Adipose tissues	
Total lipids[6,40]	25–32*
Cardiac muscle	
Total lipids[22,38]	17
Phospholipids[22,38]	16
Mitochondria[33]	
Total lipids	13
Cardiolipids	22
Phosphatidylethanolamine	29
Phosphatidylcholine	22
Embryo	
Total lipids[41]	3
Brain	
Phospholipids—cerebrosides[6]	10

* In man, 14%[5]

The intake of partially hydrogenated vegetable oils causes an accumulation of *trans* fatty acids in adipose tissues and in all lipid fractions of the body. The consequences of these observations on health are still unknown.

Trans fatty acids in the brain

Phospholipids and cerebrosides are found in large quantities in the brain. The *trans* fatty acid content of these compounds is influenced by the content in the diet. The concentrations found in the brain lipids, however, are always lower than those found in lipid fractions isolated from other organs.[40] The influence of *trans* fatty acids on brain function remains unknown.

TRANS FATTY ACIDS AND CANCER

It has been suggested on occasion that the incidence of certain types of cancer, particularly cancer of the breast and of the colon, is associated with diet. The consumption of animal fat was sometimes envisaged as one of the major causes of these two types of cancer. Unfortunately, in epidemiological studies dealing with this subject, a high intake of animal fat was also associated with certain of these diseases which are frequent in populations with a high standard of living. It should be remembered that the higher the standard of living the higher the consumption of meat and of total animal fat. Clearly it is unsound to postulate a cause-and-effect relationship in a simple mathematical correlation between the incidence of these diseases and the consumption of animal fat.

In an attempt to throw some light on such associations, Keeney and his colleagues of the University of Maryland made a study of the relationship which might be found between the consumption of vegetable and animal fats and the incidence of certain types of cancer. For this study, they used consumption data which had been used by others who had concluded that there was a correlation between the incidence of certain types of cancer and the consumption of animal fat.

The study published by Enig, Munn and Keeney[20] showed that the consumption of fat from all sources, except animal fat, had increased gradually since the beginning of the century; the consumption of animal fat, for all practical purposes, has remained stable. The increase in total fat consumption could be accounted for by an increase in the consumption of vegetable fat and partially hydrogenated oils. In fact, the consumption of total fat per capita, which was 125 g per day in 1910, rose gradually to 155 g per day in the early 70s. During that period, the consumption of animal fat remained uniform at about 100 g per day while the consumption of vegetable fat tripled. Among vegetable fats, the increase in the consumption of partially hydrogenated oils was the most marked. The overall increase in fat consumption, therefore, was due mainly to an increase in the consumption of vegetable fat and more specifically of partially hydrogenated oils.

The Maryland group[20] showed a highly significant positive correlation between death rate due to cancer of the breast and pancreas and the increasing consumption of vegetable fat. They found no correlation, however, between death rates due to these types of cancer and the consumption of animal fat. According to these calculations, therefore, the consumption of animal fat could not be the cause of the increased death rates due to these particular types of cancer.

Additional calculations using highly specialized statistical methods, showed that the increasing consumption of *trans* fatty acids could explain much of the relationship between the vegetable fat consumption trend and the incidence of the types of cancer being investigated.

Of course, the type of association suggested by mathematical correlation is open to criticism. But such criticisim could also apply to many attempts which have been made to establish an association between the incidence of many diseases and changes in food habits. Studies attempting to link the incidence of coronary heart disease to the consumption of animal fat through mathematical correlations are subject to the same criticism, because a mathematical relationship between two variables does not necessarily mean a cause-and-effect relationship.

Even if the observations of the Maryland group are based on mathematical correlations, they may serve to emphasize the fact that the consumption of animal fat is not correlated with the incidence of mortality from the types of cancer they studied. However, to those who believe that dietary fats could be responsible for the incidence of some diseases, particularly in countries with a high standard of living, the observations reported by Enig, Munn and Keeney[20] suggest that the increasing intake of *trans* fatty acids should not be ignored.

It would be difficult, with present knowledge, to explain how *trans* fatty acids could be associated with certain types of cancer. It is known, however, that the intake of partially hydrogenated oils causes the incorporation of *trans* fatty acids into all lipid fractions of the body. It is also known that these acids have physicochemical and biochemical properties which are different from their natural *cis*-isomers. In this connection, it might be important to recall that the fatty acid composition of the lipid fraction of cell membranes affects the permeability and fluidity of these membranes.[43] Let us add that the composition of the phospholipids of mitochondria isolated from cardiac muscle is greatly modified following the intake of partially hydrogenated corn oil (*see* Fig 27). In view of the fact that phospholipids make up 50–80 per cent of total lipids in biological membranes and that the nature of the constituent fatty acids determines the permeability and fluidity of these membranes, it might be suspected that the incorporation of *trans* fatty acids into phospholipids following the intake of partially hydrogenated oils might affect the normal functioning of cell membranes and as a consequence the development and proliferation of certain cancer cells. Nevertheless, for the time being, this explanation is strictly hypothetical.

TRANS FATTY ACIDS AND ATHEROSCLEROSIS

Atherosclerosis, a major cause of coronary heart disease, is characterized by lipid deposits in the arterial walls. The formation of these deposits seems to be closely associated with the normal course of life, but their cause is still unknown. In certain animal species, degenerative cells can be observed in the arterial walls of the fetus, which could be the origin of lesions leading to the formation of insoluble deposits. After birth, the incidence of this type of degenerative process increases with age.[32]

Some dietary factors are thought to accelerate the development of atherosclerosis in man. Certain saturated fatty acids are often listed among these factors. The geometrical isomers (*trans* isomers) of unsaturated fatty acids taken as margarines or shortenings based on partially hydrogenated vegetable oils, have been shown earlier in this chapter to behave like saturated fatty acids in the body. Therefore the question may be raised as to the possible influence of *trans* fatty acids on the development of atherosclerosis in man.

Some experiments have demonstrated that *trans* fatty acids, as compared to their *cis* isomers, could increase blood cholesterol both in man and in animals.[2-4] For example, when men aged 39–66 consumed 100 grams of partially hydrogenated vegetable oil per day, the equivalent of 37 g of elaidic acid (*trans*-$C18:1\Delta^9$), blood cholesterol rose rapidly by about 15 per cent, and triglycerides by 47 per cent.[2] This increase in blood lipid would be less, of course, if the intake of *trans* fatty acids were within the range of 10–12 g per day. Let us note however that these men originally had lower serum cholesterol levels than average, that is about 160 mg per 100 ml. What would be the reaction of men with higher blood cholesterol, or the long-term effect of a regular intake of *trans* fatty acids in subjects of different age groups is not known.

The influence of partially hydrogenated oils on blood cholesterol seems to be more important if the diet contains cholesterol[3]. As the diet of North Americans contains nearly 500mg of cholesterol per day, the possible influence of *trans* fatty acids on blood cholesterol in individuals consuming partially hydrogenated vegetable oils cannot be ignored.

Of course, examples of experiments in which the intake of *trans* fatty acids had no effect on blood cholesterol can be found.[44,45] In all cases, however, the negative results could be explained by either the low concentration of *trans* fatty acids in the hydrogenated oils used, or the high intake of polyunsaturated fatty acids which might have counteracted the influence of the *trans* fatty acids.

Scientific data are lacking on the possible influence of the intake of partially hydrogenated oils on the formation of atheroma and the development of atherosclerosis in man. Some observations made on pigs, however, may provide some clues in this regard. In fact, the pig appears to be a reliable animal model for studies dealing with some aspects of human physiology and metabolism. This seems to be the case in studies dealing with atherosclerosis.[46–49] Some experiments have shown that the intake of partially hydrogenated vegetable oils high in *trans* fatty acids significantly increased the frequency and size of atheroma discernible in the aorta of pigs[46,49]. It is, therefore, reasonable to believe that a diet containing large amounts of *trans* fatty acids may accelerate the development of atherosclerosis. But additional research is needed before definite conclusions can be drawn on this subject.

TRANS FATTY ACIDS AND THE ESSENTIAL FATTY ACIDS

The diet must supply a certain amount of polyunsaturated fatty acids, particularly linoleic ($C18:2\omega6$) and arachidonic ($C20:4\omega6$) acids. These fatty acids are essential nutrients because the body cannot synthesize them in sufficient quantity to meet its needs. The symptoms of essential fatty acid deficiency were described in a symposium held by the Canadian Nutrition Society in 1975.[50]

Linoleic and arachidonic acids are the two fatty acids most effective in preventing the deficiency symptoms; other polyunsaturated fatty acids are much less effective. It should be noted that both linoleic and arachidonic acids are members of the family of polyunsaturated fatty acids with a double bond between carbon 6 and carbon 7 from the methyl group; they are called the $\omega6$ polyunsaturated fatty acids.

In addition to this double bond in position $\omega6$, the essential fatty acids are characterized by a particular arrangement concerning the interval between their double bonds. This particular arrangement is illustrated in Fig 2 and is commonly designated as the *cis,cis*-methylene interrupted double bond arrangement. Therefore the essential fatty acids are of the *cis* configuration at each of their double bonds.

During the partial hydrogenation of vegetable oils, some *trans* isomers of polyunsaturated fatty acids are formed. They may belong to the $\omega6$ family, but one or two of their double bonds may have the *trans* configuration. Margarines sold in Canada may contain as much as 23 per cent of total fatty acids in the form of *trans* dienes (Figs 3 and 20). It would appear to be important to review the metabolism of these unusual substances in the body and their activity as essential fatty acids.

As seen earlier, *trans* dienes* are catabolized as sources of cellular energy through the same pathways as their natural isomers. Many exper-

---

* See Chapter 1. Trans dienes may have one or two of their double bonds with the trans configuration.

iments, however, have shown that the *trans* polyunsaturated fatty acids have no essential fatty acid activity.[51-53] *Trans* dienes can neither prevent nor cure an essential fatty acid deficiency. On the contrary, in many cases they accelerate the appearance of the deficiency symptoms and worsen the skin lesions characteristic of such a deficiency. This observation led to the concept of Physiologically Active Polyunsaturated Fatty Acid (PAPUFA). This new concept tends to differentiate the polyunsaturated fatty acids in general, meaning the fatty acids with more than one double bond and the polyunsaturated fatty acids having the physiological properties of the essential fatty acids.

The reason why the *trans* dienes do not have the physiological properties of the essential fatty acids stems from the fact that these isomers of polyunsaturated natural fatty acids are identified by the particular enzyme systems in the mitochondria responsible for the elongation of specific fatty acids. These enzyme systems add methyl groups to the polyunsaturated fatty acid with an 18 carbon chain and modify the C18:2 acids into C20:3 and/or C20:4 polyunsaturated fatty acids.[54]

This elongation of the C18 fatty acids is essential in the synthesis of prostaglandins[55,56] and other similarly important compounds such as thromboxanes[57] and leukotrienes.[58-60] The physiological and metabolic properties of prostaglandins and other similar compounds are numerous, diversified, complex and, in many cases, still poorly understood. Since the *trans* dienes retain their *trans* configuration when elongated and transformed into longer-chain fatty acids, they do not have the physiological activities characteristic of the essential fatty acids which are of the natural *cis* isomer series. The still unknown consequences to health of the formation of elongated and modified polyunsaturated *trans* fatty acids are of great concern to nutritionists at the moment.

Additional investigations are thus essential before the absolute safety and wholesomeness of *trans* dienes in the diet can be assured.

Since partially hydrogenated oils and foods based on such processed oils contain polyunsaturated fatty acids with no essential fatty acid properties, one analytical method has been proposed to determine the content of PAPUFA in processed oils. This method is based on the specific activity of a vegetable enzyme called lipoxidase and measures the essential fatty acid activity in terms of linoleic acid (C18:2ω6). The enzyme is specific for the methylene-interrupted double bond characteristic of linoleic acid. In some way, then, the lipoxidase method would measure the residual essential fatty acid (PAPUFA) content of partially hydrogenated oils and of foods processed with these oils.

In view of this, and in view of the fact that *trans* fatty acids, in some way, are metabolized like saturated fatty acids, it was of interest to reexamine some margarines as sources of physiologically active polyunsaturated fatty acids (PAPUFA). To do this, the P/S ratio—the ratio of the polyunsaturated to saturated fatty acid contents—of six margarines was recalculated using the PAPUFA content as numerator, and the saturated plus *trans* fatty acid content as denominator. Some of the calculations are given in Table 10. These few examples indicate that the P/S ratio for margarines becomes 2.6–102.0 times smaller when *trans*-isomers are regarded as saturated fatty acids.

This observation led us to examine the chemical analyses made to date on margarines sold in Canada[9,10] and to recalculate their P/S ratios taking into account their *trans* fatty acid and PAPUFA contents. It was found that, under these conditions, in 56 cases out of 100, the P/S ratio of margarines is between 1.5 and 1.8; in all other cases, less than that. Only one sample out of 100 had a P/S ratio of 2.0. The parent vegetable oils used

TABLE 10

P/S RATIOS[1] OF SOME MARGARINES CONSIDERING *TRANS* FATTY ACIDS AS SATURATED FATTY ACIDS

Based on polyunsaturated total fatty acids[2] (A)	Taking into account trans fatty acids[3] (B)	(A) (B)
3.66	0.05	73.2
3.06	0.03	102.0
1.89	0.72	2.6
1.38	0.14	9.86
1.00	0.12	8.3
0.28	0.03	9.3

[1] *Ratio of the concentrations of polyunsaturated to saturated fatty acids*
[2] *Without taking into account the trans fatty acid content*
[3] *Counting trans fatty acids as saturated fatty acids*

The analytical method commonly used for the quantitative assay of fatty acids does not distinguish between the geometrical, *cis*, and *trans*-isomers. Moreover, it does not differentiate between polyunsaturated fatty acids with the methylene-interrupted double bond, characteristic of the essential fatty acids, and other isomers without it and without the physiological activity of essential fatty acids. However, highly specialized and sophisticated methods may be used to quantify the inactive isomers. Since *trans* fatty acids in many aspects are metabolized as saturated fatty acids, and since *trans*-dienes do not have the physiological properties of essential fatty acids, it was found of interest to calculate the P/S ratio of some margarines considering *trans* fatty acids as saturates. In all cases, the P/S ratio was lowered considerably, sometimes by a factor of 100.

in the manufacture of margarine, have a P/S ratio of 3.8–6.5 before partial hydrogenation. Therefore, it may be concluded that over 50 per cent of margarines sold in Canada have a P/S ratio much closer to animal than to vegetable fats.

In conclusion, it might be said that our ignorance regarding the physiology and metabolism of the positional and geometrical isomers appearing in many foods and their long-term effects on health is deplorable. A great deal of research is still needed to answer the following questions, given as examples.

What are the long-term effects of increased intake of *trans* fatty acids on vital organ metabolism?

What are the effects of maternal dietary intake of *trans* fatty acids on the developing fetus?

What are the effects of increased intake of *trans* fatty acids on the composition and nutritive value of maternal milk?

What are the long-term effects of increased intake of *trans* fatty acids on the developing child?

What are the genetic variations in response to *trans* fatty acids in the diets of humans?

What are the long-term effects of increased intake of *trans* fatty acids on the development of atherosclerosis and perhaps on some types of cancer?

REFERENCES

1. Enig MG, Pallansch LA, Sampugna J, Keeney M: Fatty acid composition of selected food items with emphasis on *trans* octadecenoate. Paper presented at the annual meeting of the Am Oil Chem Soc, New York, April 27–May 1, 1980
2. Anderson JT, Grande F, Keys A: Hydrogenated fats in the diet and lipids in the serum of man. *J Nutr*, 75:388–394, 1961
3. Vergroesen AJ: Dietary fat and cardiovascular disease: possible modes of action of linoleic acid. *Proc Nutr Soc*, 31:323–329, 1972
4. McMillan GC, Silver MD, Weigensberg BI: Elaidinized olive oil and cholesterol atherosclerosis. *Arch Path*, 76:118–124, 1963
5. Kummerow FA: Nutrition imbalance and angiotoxins as dietary risk factors in coronary heart disease. *Am J Clin Nutr*, 32:58–83, 1979
6. Le Breton E, Lemarchal P: Les acides gras de forme *trans* en physiologie animale. *Ann Nutr Aliment*, 21:1–23, 1967
7. Watts TA, Gullett EA, Sabry JH, Liefeld JP: Tendances de la consommation alimentaire et de la nutrition au Canda. (Groupe de la politique alimentaire: Rapport.) Ministère de la Consommation et des Corporations Canada, Ottawa, October, 1977
8. Sahasrabudhe MR, Kurian CJ: Fatty acid composition of margarines in Canada. *J Inst Can Sci Technol Aliment*, 12:140–144, 1979
9. Kurian J, Sahasrabudhe MR: Fatty acid composition of margarines in Canada. *Agriculture Canada*, pp 1–73, 1979
10. Beare-Rogers JL, Gray LM, Hollywood

R: The linoleic acid and *trans* fatty acids of margarines. *Am J Clin Nutr,* 32:1805–1809, 1979

11. Dawson RMC, Kemp P: Biohydrogenation of dietary fats in ruminants. In Phillipson AT (ed) *Physiology of Digestion and Metabolism in the Ruminant,* pp 504–518 (Proceedings of the Third International Symposium, Cambridge, England). London, Oriel Press, 1969

12. Katz I, Keeney M: Characterization of the octadecenoic acids in rumen digesta and rumen bacteria. *J Dairy Sci,* 49:962–966, 1966

13. Smith LM, Dunkley WL, Franke A, Dairiki T: Measurement of *trans* and other isomeric unsaturated fatty acids in butter and margarine. *J Am Oil Chem Soc,* 55:257–261, 1978

14. Enig MG, Pallansch LA, Walker HE, Sampugna J, Keeney M: *Trans* fatty acids: concerns regarding increasing levels in the American diet and possible health implications. Maryland Nutritional Conference for Feed Manufacturers, pp 9–17. Proceedings, 1979

15. Hay JD, Morrison WR: Isomeric monoenoic fatty acids in bovine milk fat. *Biochim Biophys Acta,* 202:237–243, 1970

16. Kuzdzal-Savoie S, Raymond J: Les acides gras *trans* du beurre. I. Isolement et dosage. *Ann Biol Anim Biochim Biophys,* 5:497–511, 1965

17. Parodi PW: Distribution of isomeric octadecenoic fatty acids in milk fat. *J Dairy Sci,* 59:1870–1873, 1976

18. Enig MG: *Trans* fatty acids from different sources. Personal communication, 1979

19. Rizek RL, Friend B, Page L: Fat in today's food supply—level of use and sources. *J Am Oil Chem Soc,* 51:244–250, 1974

20. Enig MG, Munn RJ, Keeney M: Dietary fat and cancer trends—a critique. *Fed Proc,* 37:2215–2220, 1978

21. Nutrition Canada: Rapport sur les habitudes alimentaires. Ministère de la santé et du Bien-être social, January, 1977

22. Kummerow FA: Current studies on relation of fat to health. *J Am Oil Chem Soc,* 51:255–259, 1974

23. Coots RH: A comparison of the metabolism of elaidic, oleic, palmitic, and stearic acids in the rat. *J Lipid Res,* 5:468–472, 1964

24. Coots RH: A comparison of the metabolism of *cis,cis*-linoleic, *trans,trans*-linoleic, and a mixture of *cis,trans*- and *trans,cis*-linoleic acids in the rat. *J Lipid Res,* 5:473–476, 1964

25. White A, Handler P, Smith EL, Hill RL, Lehman IR: In Jeffers JD, Macnow A, LaBarbera M, Armstrong T (eds) *Principles of Biochemistry* (ed 6). New York, McGraw-Hill Book Company, 1978

26. Ono K, Fredrickson DS: The metabolism of ^{14}C-labeled *cis* and *trans* isomers of octadecenoic and octadecadienoic acids. *J Biol Chem,* 239:2482–2488, 1964

27. Anderson RL: Oxidation of the geometric isomers of $\Delta^{9,12}$-octadecadienoic acid by rat liver mitochondria. *Biochim Biophys Acta,* 152:531–538, 1968

28. Willebrands AF, Van der Veen KJ: The metabolism of elaidic acid in the perfused rat heart. *Biochim Biophys Acta,* 116:583–585, 1966

29. Anderson RL, Coots RH: The catabolism of the geometric isomers of uniformly ^{14}C-labeled Δ^{9}-octadecenoic acid and uniformly ^{14}C-labeled $\Delta^{9,12}$-octadecadienoic acid by the fasting rat. *Biochim Biophys Acta,* 144:525–531, 1967

30. Lawson LD, Kummerow FA: β-oxidation of the coenzyme A esters of vaccenic, elaidic, and petroselaidic acids by rat heart mitochondria. *Lipids,* 14:501–503, 1979

31. Lawson LD, Kummerow FA: β-oxidation of the coenzyme A esters of elaidic, oleic, and stearic acids and their full-cycle intermediates by rat heart mitochondria. *Biochim Biophys Acta,* 573:245–254, 1979

32. Kummerow FA: Effects of isomeric fats on animal tissue, lipid classes, and

atherosclerosis. In Emken EA, Dutton HJ (eds) *Geometrical and Positional Fatty Acid Isomers*, pp 151–179. Illinois, American Oil Chemists' Society, Monograph 6, 1979

33. Hsu CML, Kummerow FA: Influence of elaidate and erucate on heart mitochondria. *Lipids*, 12:486–494, 1977

34. Schrock CG, Connor WE: Incorporation of the dietary *trans* fatty acid (C18:1) into the serum lipids, the serum lipoproteins and adipose tissue. *Am J Clin Nutr*, 28:1020–1027, 1975

35. Lands WEM, Blank ML, Nutter LJ, Privett OS: A comparison of acyltransferase activities *in vitro* with the distribution of fatty acids in lecithins and triglycerides *in vivo*. *Lipids*, 1:224–229, 1966

36. Sgoutas DS: Hydrolysis of synthetic cholesterol esters containing *trans* fatty acids. *Biochim Biophys Acta*, 164:317–326, 1968

37. Egwim PO, Kummerow FA: Influence of dietary fat on the concentration of long-chain unsaturated fatty acid families in rat tissues. *J Lipid Res*, 13:500–510, 1972

38. Egwim PO, Kummerow FA: Incorporation and distribution of dietary elaidate in the major lipid classes of rat heart and plasma lipoprotein. *J Nutr*, 102:783–792, 1972

39. Egwim PO, Sgoutas DS: Occurrence of eicosadienoic acids in liver lipids of rats fed partially hydrogenated soybean fat. *J Nutr*, 101:307–314, 1971

40. Decker WJ, Mertz W: Incorporation of dietary elaidic acid in tissues and effects on fatty acid distribution. *J Nutr*, 89:165–170, 1966

41. Pallansch LA, Tidler LM, Sampugna J, Keeney M: Occurrence of *trans* fatty acids in newborn mice. Paper presented at the annual meeting of The Am Oil Chem Soc, New York, April 27–May 1, 1980

42. Jensen RG, Clark RM, Ferris AM: Composition of the lipids in human milk: A review. *Lipids*, 15:345–355, 1980

43. Vigo C, Goni FM, Quinn PJ, Chapman D: The modulation of membrane fluidity by hydrogenation processes. II.

Homogeneous catalysis and model biomembranes. *Biochim Biophys Acta*, 508:1–14, 1978

44. Erickson AB, Coots RH, Mattson FH, Kligman AM: The effect of partial hydrogenation of dietary fats, of the ratio of polyunsaturated to saturated fatty acids, and of dietary cholesterol upon plasma lipids in man. *J Clin Invest*, 43:2017–2025, 1964

45. Mattson FH, Hollenbach EJ, Kligman AM: Effect of hydrogenated fat on the plasma cholesterol and triglyceride levels of man. *Am J Clin Nutr*, 28:726–731, 1975

46. Rapacz J, Elson CE, Lalich JJ: Correlation of an immunogenetically defined lipoprotein type with aortic intimal lipidosis in swine. *Exp Mol Path*, 27:249–261, 1977

47. Taura S, Taura M, Imai H, Kummerow FA: Coronary atherosclerosis in normocholesterolemic swine. *Artery*, 4:395–407, 1978

48. Kummerow FA, Cho BHS, Huang WYT, Imai H, Kamio A, Deutsch MJ, Hooper WM: Additive risk factors in atherosclerosis. *Am J Clin Nutr*, 29:579–584, 1976

49. Kummerow FA, Mizuguchi T, Arima T, Cho BHS, Huang WYT: The influence of three sources of dietary fats and cholesterol on lipid composition of swine serum lipids and aorta tissue. *Artery*, 4:360–384, 1978

50. Holman RT: Deficiency of essential fatty acids in humans. In Hawkins WW (ed) *The Essential Fatty Acids. Proceedings of the Miles Symposium '75 presented by The Nutrition Society of Canada, June 23, 1975*, pp 45–58. Winnipeg, Manitoba, University of Manitoba, 1976

51. Aaes-Jøgensen E: Certain aspects of polyunsaturated fatty acids in nutrition. In Somogyi JC, François A (eds) *Nutritional Aspects of Fats*, pp 17–23. Bibliotheca Nutritio et Dieta, no 25. Series of the Institute for Nutrition Research, vol. 25. Basel, Karger, 1977

52. Renner R: Nutritive value of *trans* fatty acids. Personal communication, Human Nutrition Committee, 1979

53. Privett OS, Phillips F, Shimasaki H, Nozawa T, Nickell EC: Studies of effects of *trans* fatty acids in the diet on lipid metabolism in essential fatty acid deficient rats. *Am J Clin Nutr,* 30:1009–1017, 1977

54. Privett OS, Stearns EM Jr, Nickell EC: Metabolism of the geometric isomers of linoleic acid in the rat. *J Nutr,* 92:303–310, 1967

55. Samuelsson B, Paoletti R: In Samuelsson B, Paoletti R (eds) *Advances in prostaglandin and thromboxane research,* Vols 1 and 2. New York, Raven Press, 1976

56. Curtis-Prior PB: *Prostaglandins. An introduction to their biochemistry, physiology and pharmacology.* New York, North-Holland, 1976

57. Kolata GB: Thromboxanes: The power behind the prostaglandins? *Science,* 190:770–771, 812, 1975

58. Murphy RC, Hammarström S, Samuelsson B: Leukotriene C: A slow-reacting substance from murine mastocytoma cells. *Proc Natl Acad Sci U.S.A,* 76:4275–4279, 1979

59. Hammarström S, Murphy RC, Samuelsson B, Clark DA, Mioskowski C, Corey EJ: Structure of leukotriene C identification of the amino acid part. *Biochem Biophys Res Comm,* 91:1266–1272, 1979

60. Corey EJ, Clark DA, Goto G, Marfat A, Mioskowski C, Samuelsson B, Hammarström S: Stereospecific total synthesis of a "slow reacting substance" of anaphlaxis, leukotriene C-1. *J Am Chem Soc,* 102:1436–1439, 1980

4
Cholesterophobia

INTRODUCTION

Cholesterol, as was described earlier, is a substance essential to life*. It is found in all cells of the body and it plays a basic role both as a precursor molecule of hormones and other major molecules and as a structural element of membranes. Yet in the general public such a phobia about this vital substance has been induced that instead of being regarded as an essential substance it is regarded rather with an element of fear.

This situation is due to the facts:

(1)   that the presence of cholesterol in blood serum has been seen as a risk factor for cardiovascular disease; and
(2)   that certain epidemiological studies have found an association between the consumption of foodstuffs rich in cholesterol and the mortality from that disease.

Yet, in spite of a wealth of investigations on the subject, it is still uncertain whether cholesterol is truly a cause of cardiovascular disease in man. It is also uncertain whether a reduction in the consumption of food rich in cholesterol would result in a reduction in mortality due to this disease.

The fear and uncertainty about cholesterol have caused a controversy dividing physicians, nutritionists and others into two main groups. On one hand, there are those who support the *lipid* hypothesis and believe that the consumption of food rich in cholesterol is a major cause of cardiovascular disease. On the other hand, there are those who consider that scientific evidence is still insufficient to recommend major changes in dietary habits aimed at reducing blood cholesterol levels. Our intention is not to

---

* See Chapter 1.

settle this controversy, but to analyse the most recent data and help the reader to develop a well-balanced opinion on the matter.

BLOOD CHOLESTEROL AS A RISK FACTOR FOR CORONARY HEART DISEASE

Coronary heart disease is still the major cause of mortality in industrialized countries. One characteristic of this disease is that it is insidious and sometimes strikes, fatally, without warning. A number of persons who recover from their first attack remain disabled for the rest of their life. The burden of this disease in our society is considerable; thus it is important to determine the most effective ways for its prevention.

From the available information, diseases generally labeled as coronary heart diseases (CHD) are closely associated with atherosclerosis, a condition which may lead to the complete occlusion of vital arteries. Atherosclerosis develops over the course of several years with no indication of the potential severity of an attack.

To counter this condition effectively, methods to identify susceptible individuals must be available or alternatively preventive measures which can be adopted by the entire population must be developed.

The first indication that cholesterol might be involved in the development of atherosclerosis came from experiments carried out with rabbits fed a high cholesterol diet. These studies were conducted in Russia at the beginning of the century[1]. Post-mortem lesions similar to those encountered in human atherosclerosis were observed in the intima of the aorta. Control animals which received no cholesterol in their diet were free from such lesions. In other experiments, rabbits fed meat, milk or eggs, all of which contain cholesterol, also developed arterial lesions typical of atherosclerosis. Since then, many investigations on rabbits and other animal species confirmed these initial observations. As a result of these studies, a hypothesis was put forward that may be stated as follows:

The development of atherosclerosis in man is causally associated with the level of cholesterol in blood, which in turn is influenced by the intake of foods high in cholesterol.

This hypothesis has influenced many investigators, but the experimental evidence on which it is based, being derived from experimental animals, was often inapplicable to man. For example, it is well known that the rabbit is particularly sensitive to dietary cholesterol so that observations obtained with this animal cannot be applied to man. The rabbit is a herbivorous animal and its normal diet contains no cholesterol. Accordingly, its physiology evolved without exposure to dietary cholesterol and did not develop the particular control mechanisms observed in man and other omnivorous species which maintain cholesterol homeostasis. It is evident, then, that the rabbit is not an animal of choice for studies on the role of dietary cholesterol in the development of atherosclerosis; it is also obvious that the results obtained with this animal are not applicable to man.

Keeping the above hypothesis in mind[2], even if it is not universally accepted[3], let us first examine the data published by Kannel in 1976[4] which illustrate the type of correlation observed between total cholesterol in blood serum and the probability that men 30–49 years of age will develop clinical coronary disease (Fig 28).

The distribution of values in Fig 28 is typical of many biological relationships. At a serum cholesterol level below 200 mg per 100 ml, the

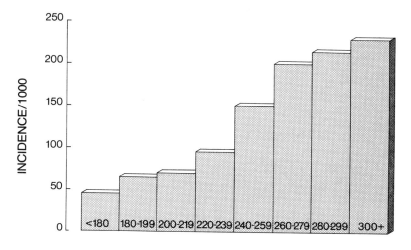

SERUM CHOLESTEROL (mg/100ml)

Fig. 28—Relationship between serum cholesterol level and the frequency of coronary disease in men 30–49 years of age.

(Adapted from Kannel[4].)

This histogram was based on data collected during the important Framingham study. It shows a mathematical correlation between serum cholesterol and the risk of coronary disease. Because of the nature of the relationship, the point on the graph where blood cholesterol is closely associated with the risk is considerably reduced. Yet within this same region a change of only 40 per cent in serum cholesterol is associated with a rise of 400 per cent in risk. This phenomenon greatly jeopardizes the accuracy of the prediction when it is applied to a given person selected at random within the population. Note also that this histogram simply illustrates a mathematical relationship.

frequency of coronary disease remains low and varies little. Above 200 mg per 100 ml the frequency increases rapidly up to 280 mg, where a plateau is reached. In other words, the risk is about 3–4 times higher among men with a concentration of 280 mg per 100 ml than it is among those with 200 mg per 100 ml. As a result, for an increase of only 40 per cent in serum cholesterol, the risk increases by a factor of about 400 per cent. Under such conditions, a disproportionately high variation is to be expected in the predicted risk as compared to the low variation in serum cholesterol. Such a relationship between the two variables reduces greatly the precision with which the risk of coronary disease may be evaluated for a given individual chosen at random.

This lack of accuracy might be acceptable if the analytical technique for measuring serum cholesterol were not subject to serious experimental errors and, occasionally, considerable laboratory to laboratory variation. Variations in serum cholesterol as large as 30 to 50 mg per 100 ml have been observed, depending on the analytical method used[5]. These errors alone may raise or lower the apparent risk by a factor of 200–250 per cent.

The meaningfulness of the association between serum cholesterol and the risk of coronary disease also depends greatly on the manner in which serum cholesterol varies in the normal population. To evaluate the extent of the variation in the normal population, we have drawn the so-called normal distribution curve for serum cholesterol in the United States of America. The curve is based on five major investigations summarized in 1979 by Stamler[6], and referred to as the Framingham, Albany, Chicago Gas, Chicago W.E. and Tecumseh studies.

It is seen (Fig 29) that serum cholesterol in the average American adult ranges from 140 mg per 100 ml to more than 355 mg, an interval of 215 mg; the highest concentration exceeds the lowest by a factor of 255 per cent. Because of this large difference in values, the distribution curve shows wide variations about the mean value which is 234 mg per 100 ml as reported by Stamler[6]. Variation about the mean can be calculated and is expressed by a value called the standard deviation. The standard deviation for the mean concentration of serum cholesterol reported for the populations represented in Fig 29 is 45 mg per 100 ml[6]. An interpretation of this value, based on the most elementary principles of biostatistics, may be stated as follows:

> 66 per cent of adult U.S. citizens would normally have serum cholesterol levels varying between 190 and 280 mg per 100 ml (mean ± one standard deviation).

The standard deviation (σ) for the distribution curve illustrated in Fig 29 also means that only about 17 per cent of the adult population would have a serum cholesterol level exceeding 280 mg per 100 ml, and 17 per cent would have a concentration of less than 190 mg. It is clear that serum

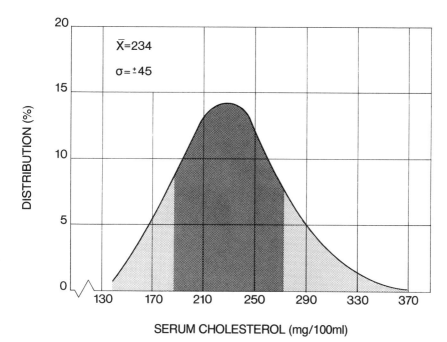

Fig. 29—Distribution curve of serum cholesterol in the population of the United States.

(Prepared from data reported by Stamler[6].)

Biostatisticians use this type of curve to show how biological parameters are distributed in the population in general. In this case, it represents the distribution of serum cholesterol in the adult population of the United States. It can be seen that the concentrations vary from 140 to more than 355 mg per 100 ml of serum, an interval of 255 per cent. The mean value is 234 mg per 100 ml with a standard deviation of 45 mg per 100 ml. According to biostatisticians an interpretation of this standard deviation is that 66 per cent of adults in the United States would normally have serum cholesterol levels varying between 190 and 280 mg per 100 ml; only 17 per cent would have a concentration exceeding 280 mg per 100 ml.

cholesterol varies considerably in adult populations with dietary habits such as those of Americans. Such a wide variation makes it difficult, if not impossible, to set the limits within which given levels of serum cholesterol might be considered truly normal. The meaningfulness of the relationship between serum cholesterol and the risk of coronary heart disease is thus greatly reduced by the wide variations normally observed in the adult population.

It is also known, of course, that the serum cholesterol level varies with age and sex. Recent data[7] show that the mean cholesterol level is 190 mg per 100 ml for men between 18 and 24 years of age, but is as high as 240 mg in men 45–54 years old; this concentration is maintained until at least the age of 75. In women, the corresponding concentrations are 190 mg per 100 ml for the age group 18–24 and 240 mg per 100 ml for the group 45–54 years of age; there is a continuing increase up to the age of 65 and 75. Nevertheless, the normal distribution curve at all ages and for both sexes is identical to that illustrated in Fig 29; this means that the extent of the variation about the mean value will still be considerable and that comments on distribution similar to those made above would not be unacceptable. These observations make it difficult to interpret the serum cholesterol level in a given individual with regard to the risk of coronary heart disease.

Under these conditions, the following question would seem in order: what really should be considered the normal concentration of serum cholesterol in the adult American citizen? In this regard, there are serious differences of opinion: is it 250 mg per 100 ml, is it 300 mg, who knows? This question becomes more complex when the notion of optimum and desirable concentrations is added to that of a normal level[5]. Furthermore, a normal, desirable and optimum concentration varies with sex, age, previous medical record, family case history, proneness to coronary heart disease and other factors. In view of these uncertainties, which are further complicated by the unreliability of risk-prediction, errors in analytical methods, normal variations in serum cholesterol concentration and lack of consensus with respect to normal, optimal and desirable serum cholesterol levels, Carlson[3] wrote in 1979: *"Let total serum-cholesterol be retired after its long service"*. That could be the end of the controversy concerning serum cholesterol!

The kind of relationship just described and illustrated in Fig 28 between the cholesterol concentration in blood serum and the risk of cardiovascular disease has been confirmed by many epidemiological studies, and in this regard, there has been no disagreement[8-15]. Yet, interpreting that relationship as one of cause-and-effect would be a serious error. Epidemiologists, biostatisticians and nutritionists who studied this relationship generally acknowledged that it is simply a mathematical relationship and perhaps a matter of chance, even though, according to biostatisticians, it is a mathematically highly significant one. The fact that two variables vary in parallel does not necessarily mean that a cause-and-effect relationship exists between them.

Biostatisticians always caution against a cause-and-effect interpretation when a significant correlation is observed between two variables. The correlation coefficient is simply a mathematical expression of parallelism between two variables progressing in the same or in the opposite direction.

If the coefficient is positive and if it is significant from the biostatistical standpoint, it means that the two variables actually move in the same direction. Of course it is often difficult to accept that a positive correlation coefficient may not be a satisfactory explanation for a given phenomenon, especially if this correlation confirms a theory to which we subscribe. Cholesterophobia is largely accounted for by the fact that the relationship was too rapidly accepted as a cause-and-effect one. The belief that blood cholesterol is the cause of atherosclerosis still persists in the population at large; cholesterol is identified with cardiovascular disease.

The lipid hypothesis as described by Ahrens[16] was effectively based on the type of observation described above and illustrated in Fig 28. The lipid hypothesis is the postulate that "...reducing the level of plasma cholesterol in an individual or in a population group will lead to a reduction in the risk of suffering a new event of coronary heart disease."[16]

This hypothesis went far beyond the initial mathematical relationship and led to the postulate that a reduction in serum cholesterol in an individual picked at random within the population would result in a reduction of the risk of cardiovascular disease. This postulate implies a cause-and-effect interpretation of the mathematical relationship between serum cholesterol and the incidence of coronary heart disease. Ahrens himself states that this postulate has never been proved to be true "to the satisfaction of epidemiologists or of biostatisticians or of the medical community"[16]. One could add: "or of nutritionists, animal scientists or the scientific community". Dr. Ahrens continues: "Even though the lipid hypothesis has been tested over and over again in the past two decades, it has been impossible to obtain satisfactory proof for or against".

> *Those who take action and make recommendations as if the lipid hypothesis has been verified are in danger of making a serious mistake. Meanwhile, for the man in the street, cholesterol has become synonymous with cardiovascular disease. Publicity to this effect has been such that it will take several years before this popular belief is corrected.*

EFFECT OF DIETARY CHOLESTEROL ON SERUM CHOLESTEROL

If it were true that cholesterol is the major agent in the etiology of atherosclerosis and cardiovascular disease, a small decrease in serum cholesterol would correspond to a significant reduction in the incidence of the disease. If the relationship between serum cholesterol and the risk of coronary disease were one of cause-and-effect, it would surely merit the full attention that it gets; and public health measures aimed at reducing the concentration of serum cholesterol in the population in general would be justified. For this reason, the lipid hypothesis even if it has not yet been scientifically proven still exerts its influence in many circles where food and nutrition policies are elaborated. For that reason, it would appear advisable to review some of the factors thought to influence the serum cholesterol level in man.

Most investigations dealing with the possible influence of dietary cholesterol on serum cholesterol levels have been made in the belief that the cholesterol level in blood is closely linked with the development of atherosclerosis and the risk of cardiovascular disease. This led to the lipid hypothesis, as described by Ahrens[16], and to the further postulate that an overall decrease of blood cholesterol in a given population would mean a significant decrease in cardiovascular problems in the individuals of that population. In this context, a study on the possible relationship between dietary cholesterol and blood cholesterol should be of great significance.

Generally, tests made on animals have shown a close correlation between dietary cholesterol and the serum cholesterol level. The first experiments which were carried out at the beginning of the century on rabbits fed meat, milk and eggs remain classics[1]. These studies showed effectively that the concentration of cholesterol in blood rose markedly when rabbits consumed foodstuffs high in cholesterol. The many studies made with the rabbit model and with other animal species gave similar results.

Today, however, it is generally recognized that man's response to dietary cholesterol is quite different from that of most animal species, especially the rabbit. Accordingly, the results obtained with animals should not be extrapolated to man. That is why in this book, we restrict ourselves to investigations carried out on man and we draw special attention to the most recent publications.

Let us first identify three types of studies: (a) Epidemiological studies made on populations generally quite different from one another; (b) investigations made on sub-groups of populations considered as homogeneous, and (c) studies made on individuals fed controlled diets.

Epidemiological studies in different countries

Many major epidemiological studies have been carried out in the past two decades. Generally, all were probably inspired by the corollary to the lipid hypothesis, the assumption that there is a correlation between dietary cholesterol and serum cholesterol levels.

A study of the postulated relationship between dietary cholesterol and the incidence of coronary heart disease in twenty countries is summarized in Fig 30. The data reported by Stamler[6] were used to prepare this figure. A straight line can be drawn, as shown, to indicate a correlation between dietary cholesterol and the mortality due to cardiovascular disease. In fact, a statistically significant correlation can be shown between these two variables.

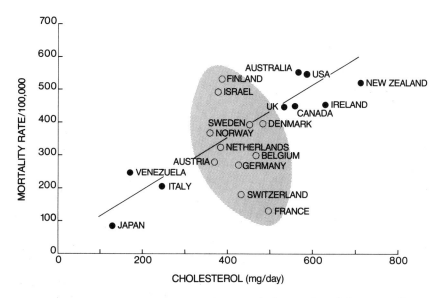

Fig. 30—Relationship between dietary cholesterol and the mortality rate due to coronary heart disease.

(Based on data reported by Stamler[6] using the 1971 and 1973 CHD mortality rates for men and women.)

Many major epidemiological studies were carried out during the last two decades in an attempt to define the relationship between the consumption of foods high in cholesterol and the mortality rate due to coronary heart disease. This figure gives an example of this relationship as observed in twenty countries. Applying the principles of biostatistics, it appears that only 36 per cent of the variation in mortality could be accounted for by dietary cholesterol; 64 per cent would be due to other variables. In eleven countries, more than half, the correlation between dietary cholesterol and mortality is in fact negative. For these countries, therefore, there would be no apparent association between dietary cholesterol and coronary heart disease mortality. Too many similar studies were used in trying to establish a cause-and-effect relationship between dietary cholesterol and the mortality rate due to coronary heart disease; it should always be kept in mind that the kind of relationship illustrated in this figure is simply a mathematical one and as such is not a proof that the one effect causes the other.

Let us examine closely some characteristics of this relationship. Firstly, the correlation coefficient between these two variables throughout these twenty countries is only 0.6. Such a correlation coefficient is highly significant according to biostatistical methods, but what it really means is that only 36 per cent of the variation in mortality is accounted for by dietary cholesterol. As a result, 64 per cent of the variation is necessarily attributable to other variables. Furthermore, one can estimate from Fig 30 that in eleven of the twenty countries (○), cholesterol intake ranges from 358 to 481 mg per day, equivalent to only 15.7 per cent of the full range of intakes for all countries, whereas the mortality rate ranges from 87 to 533 per 100,000, or 84 per cent of the full range for this variable. The elliptical area which covers these eleven countries actually shows that for these countries, the correlation between dietary cholesterol and mortality is in fact negative. Thus, it may be stated that for more than half of the countries in Fig 30 there is no apparent association between dietary cholesterol and the mortality due to coronary heart disease.

The words "highly significant" mentioned previously as applied to a correlation coefficient do not necessarily mean that the association between the two variables concerned is causal. Yet, this kind of relationship is often used to illustrate the causative role of dietary cholesterol in coronary heart disease. All professionals interested in the role of lipids in human nutrition should be alerted so that the type of association illustrated in Fig 30 is not misused and interpreted as establishing a definite cause-and-effect relationship.

The tenuousness of the association between dietary cholesterol and coronary heart disease, as represented in Fig 30, is such that the relationship loses much of its significance when other factors that might be associated with it are considered. As a matter of fact, one may calculate other significant correlation coefficients between other factors equally possibly associated with coronary heart disease.

Such coefficients have been calculated by Stamler[6]. It can thus be observed that a significant correlation coefficient* exists between the consumption of meat and sugar ($r = 0.77$), between the consumption of total fats and cholesterol ($r = 0.83$), between smoking and the intake of cholesterol ($r = 0.73$), between the average annual income per capita and dietary cholesterol ($r = 0.59$), and so on. The correlation coefficient is also significant between the total intake in calories and the consumption of meat, eggs and sugar. Examining further such relationships, one finds that the consumption of total fats, saturated fatty acids, meat and eggs is as closely associated with the average annual per capita income as is the consumption of cholesterol with heart disease.

Many other studies confirmed this kind of multiple association between various consumables and the mortality due to coronary heart diseases. In this regard, the thirty-seven countries study reported by Masironi[17] in 1970 and the thirty countries study reported by Armstrong et al[18] in 1975 should be mentioned.

---

* As the correlation coefficient (r) approaches 1.0 the relationship becomes closer and closer.

Among these multiple associations, how can one distinguish between those which truly affect mortality due to coronary heart disease and those which do not? Stamler himself expressed the opinion that simple mathematical associations of the nature discussed above have no significance at all from the biological point of view[6]. It is therefore logical to assume that the simple mathematical correlations between different consumables, where many items varied in close association with one another, have no practical significance in determining the causative agents of coronary heart disease.

Indeed, biostatisticians have mathematical tools, such as multiple regression analysis or multivariate analysis, to distinguish from among many variables those which are likely to be more closely correlated with coronary heart disease mortality. The use and interpretation of the data obtained with such tools, however, are difficult and require advanced training in biostatistics. Nevertheless, when these methods have been used the results have again confirmed the tenuous nature of the relationship between dietary cholesterol and coronary heart disease.

When these highly sophisticated tools were used, it was found that the relationship assumed to exist between the consumption of foods containing cholesterol and coronary heart disease mortality did not hold true. As an example, let us examine the results of a study made in Japan[19]. The intake of cholesterol in that country was 93 mg per day in 1950 and gradually rose to 381 mg per day in 1973. During the same period, the total consumption of fats and saturated fats in particular also rose significantly. But applying the appropriate statistical analyses to deal with the multiple variables involved in the study, led to the conclusion that the increase in dietary cholesterol and consumption of saturated fats during the same period had had little influence on the incidence of coronary heart disease.

Another example may be drawn from the thirty countries study[18]. In this study, it was shown first that a simple significant biostatistical correlation existed between the consumption of eggs, meat, milk and saturated fats, and the mortality due to heart disease. Further analysis of the data, however, showed that sugar consumption and smoking were also significantly correlated with the mortality from heart disease. When these correlations were analyzed[18], taking into account the effects of sugar consumption and of smoking, the authors found that other correlations, originally significant, became non-significant. This was particularly true when applied to the consumption of eggs, meat, milk, saturated fats and even total fats as seen in Table 11. Eggs, for example, are very high in cholesterol; one egg yolk contains an average of 250 mg of cholesterol. The degree of association between the consumption of eggs and the mortality was 31 per cent when simple correlation was applied, but this figure drops to 8 per cent when the association was corrected for the consumption of sugar and for smoking.

TABLE 11

DEGREE OF ASSOCIATION BETWEEN THE INCIDENCE OF MORTALITY FROM HEART DISEASE AND THE USE OF CERTAIN CONSUMER GOODS

(Adapted from data reported by Armstrong et al[18].)

Consumer goods	Degree of association (%)	Degree of association corrected for the consumption of sugar and for smoking (%)
Saturated fats	50*	6
Total fats	35*	1
Meat	42*	9
Milk	52*	0
Eggs	31*	8
Smoking	17*	—
Sugar	58*	—

* Statistically significant relationship

When correlations were calculated to take into account the effects of the consumption of sugar and of smoking on coronary heart disease mortality, other correlations, originally significant became non-significant. The data in this Table were adapted in an attempt to express more clearly the meaning of such statistical calculations.

When it is considered that the association between coronary heart disease mortality and the consumption of food items rich in cholesterol becomes non-significant, even almost nil, when corrected by multivariate analysis and that most major recent studies point in this same direction, one may conclude that the results of the major epidemiological studies:

(a) give little support to the lipid hypothesis; and
(b) give no support to a cause-and-effect relationship between the intake of dietary cholesterol and coronary heart disease mortality[20].

Studies with sub-groups in given populations

The influence of dietary cholesterol on the concentration of cholesterol in blood serum has been studied over and over again in different sub-groups. Some of these studies go as far back as the 1950s, for example Keys' study[21] published in 1956. Based on measurements of serum cholesterol and calculations of dietary cholesterol intakes, he and his colleagues came to the conclusion that:

> ". . . in the adult men the serum cholesterol level is essentially independent of the cholesterol intake over the whole range of natural human diets. It is probable that infants, children and women are similar."[21]

Fig 31 exemplifies this phenomenon. It can be seen that an increase in dietary cholesterol by a factor of 250 per cent has no significant influence on serum cholesterol level.

Investigators publishing on the same subject between 1950 and 1970 came to the same conclusion, namely that dietary cholesterol has no influence on serum cholesterol[22–26]. In 1970, the results of the important Framingham study confirmed the fact that the daily cholesterol intake had no influence on the cholesterol concentration in blood serum (Table 12). In men and women, the serum cholesterol concentration was found to be

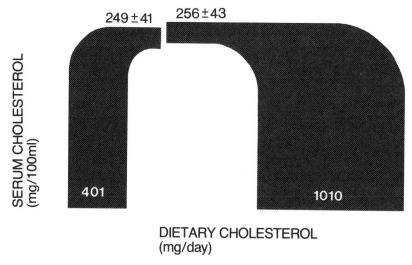

Fig. 31—*Dietary cholesterol and serum cholesterol levels in 50-year old businessmen and professionals.*

(Based on data reported by Keys *et al*[21].)

Increasing the dietary cholesterol intake by a factor of 250 per cent (401 mg vs 1,010 mg per day) had no effect on serum cholesterol levels. This investigation was carried out with 50-year old businessmen and professionals living in Minnesota, U.S.A. All these men were healthy according to the usual criteria whatever their serum cholesterol levels. Dietary cholesterol thus has no effect on blood cholesterol.

TABLE 12

CHOLESTEROL INTAKE AND BLOOD CHOLESTEROL LEVEL*

| | Cholesterol intake (mg per day) | | Serum cholesterol (mg per 100 ml) | |
Group	Average	Range	Intake of cholesterol —below mean value—	Intake of cholesterol —above mean value—
Men	704	250 to 1500	237	237
Women	492	150 to 1300	245	241

* Adapted from Kannel and Gordon[29] as quoted by Mann[30] and McGill[20]

> In the Framingham study, men and women with a dietary choles-
> terol intake higher than the mean value had the same amount of
> cholesterol in their blood as those who consumed less. These data
> greatly helped to disprove the suggestion that dietary cholesterol
> has an influence on blood cholesterol levels. In spite of these
> irrefutable observations, known for several years, the public at
> large still fears the effects of cholesterol in food.

the same whatever the intake of cholesterol in foods. The Framingham
data were similar to those presented in Fig 31 and show also that in the
population at large dietary cholesterol has no influence on serum cholesterol levels.

Furthermore this absence of correlation between the intake of dietary
cholesterol and blood cholesterol may also be observed in children. An
early study[27] dealt with children 7–12 years old whose cholesterol intake
ranged from 150 to 394 mg per day. In a second study[28] carried out with
9–11-year old children, dietary cholesterol ranged from 0 to 1,536 mg per
day. In both instances the amount of cholesterol ingested in the foods had
no effect whatsoever on the cholesterol concentration in the blood serum
of these children.

The Tecumseh (Michigan) study[31], involving 1082 women and 957
men, merits attention. The average daily cholesterol intake of the subjects
was calculated and was found to be 328 mg for women and 551 mg for men.
At the same time, their serum cholesterol levels were measured and, on
the basis of these values, the subjects were allocated to one of three
groups—high, medium and low serum cholesterol. It was found that the
intake of cholesterol was the same in the three groups despite the differences in their blood cholesterol (Fig 32).

> The conclusion is self-evident: once again, the cholesterol concen-
> tration in blood serum varied independently of dietary cholesterol.
> Therefore in the population at large, dietary cholesterol would not be
> the main factor controlling the serum cholesterol level.

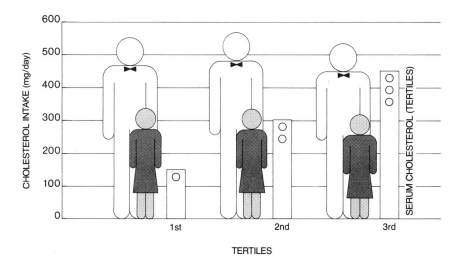

Fig. 32—Serum cholesterol under conditions of varying dietary cholesterol intake.

(Adapted from data reported by Nichols *et al*[31].)

The Tecumseh (Michigan) study dealt with 1,082 women and 957 men. The average daily cholesterol intake was nearly 330 mg per day for women and 550 mg for men. To illustrate the results, cholesterol concentrations in blood serum were grouped according to level in first, second and third tertiles. The results show that for both sexes serum cholesterol ranged from the lowest to the highest tertile, even though dietary cholesterol remained uniform. The conclusion is obvious: blood cholesterol varies independently from dietary cholesterol; in other words, in the population in general, dietary cholesterol is not the principal element that controls the concentration of cholesterol in blood.

The same conclusion was reached following studies involving a large number of subjects in Puerto Rico[32], in Honolulu[33] and elsewhere[34]. The results of all these studies allow us to conclude that:

in a homogeneous population, dietary cholesterol has no effect on the concentration of cholesterol in blood serum.

Controlled experiments with humans

The investigations summarized above were epidemiological in nature and dealt with large populations or population sub-groups; in this kind of study, the influence of dietary cholesterol is often confounded with other variables such as smoking, consumption of sugar and so forth. One still

may ask whether the intake of cholesterol has any effect on blood cholesterol in controlled experiments in humans. McGill[20] made an exhaustive
review of such investigations. The following is based on his 1979 publication.

It is interesting to note that the egg was the main source of dietary
cholesterol in nearly all investigations reported. Indeed, the egg contains
an average of 250 mg of cholesterol and it is easy to add it to or withold
it from a normal diet. In some experiments, however, crystalline cholesterol was used.

Several facts become apparent from these experiments and can be
summarized as follows.

* Disparity and inconsistency of results occurred from one experiment
   to another.
* Extreme variations were evident from one person to another in response to dietary cholesterol.
* Contradictory results occurred, depending on whether the persons
   selected were patients maintained in institutions or free-living
   individuals.
* Obvious adaptation responses were evident as the experiments
   progressed.
* There was lack of any effect when the cholesterol intake exceeded
   a certain level, about 350–400 mg per day.
* Rise or fall of serum cholesterol levels rarely exceeded 10 per cent
   of the value found in control subjects.
* There was absence of any effect when experimental subjects were
   healthy and selected from the general public.

Certain of these observations are of major importance in the formu-
lation of nutritional policies and in the choice of recommendations for the
general population.

Let us first examine the extreme variations observed from one individual to another when a change is made in the intake of dietary cholesterol.
An experiment carried out in the Netherlands[35] on 44 volunteers, 19 women
and 25 men, selected from the general public deserves our attention. These
subjects accepted a reduction to zero in their consumption of eggs which
was 9–10 per week before the experiment. This was a reduction in dietary
cholesterol of about 500 mg per day. Despite this drastic reduction in
dietary cholesterol, their serum cholesterol level dropped by only 7.1 mg
per 100 ml in men and 5.0 mg per 100 ml in women, a statistically non-
significant reduction, which means that the change observed in serum
cholesterol could have been due to chance alone.

But what is remarkable in this experiment is the great variation which
was observed from one person to another (Fig 33). Having stopped consuming eggs for three weeks, 16 persons out of 44, that is more than one
third, experienced a rise rather than a reduction in their serum cholesterol

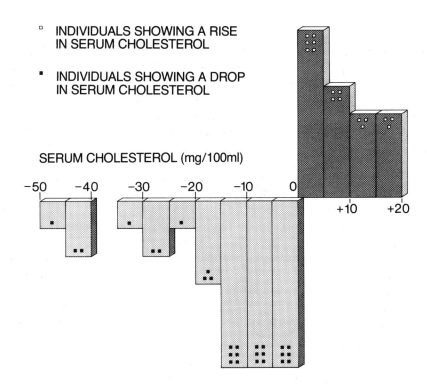

Fig. 33—*Effect of a sudden change in dietary cholesterol on serum cholesterol levels in different individuals.*

(Prepared from data reported by Bronsgeest-Schoute *et al*[35].)

In an experiment carried out in the Netherlands, 44 persons agreed to stop their weekly consumption of 9–10 eggs. After three weeks, 16 subjects (more than one third) saw their serum cholesterol level rise rather than fall, as would be expected from the lipid hypothesis. In some cases, the rise reached 10 per cent of the initial value. Among the subjects who experienced a reduction in their blood cholesterol, 21 out of 28 (75 per cent) observed a drop of less than 20 mg per 100 ml, or less than 10 per cent of the initial value. Variations of this order demonstrate the great difference which can be expected from one person to another in response to drastic changes in dietary cholesterol. Furthermore, such variations render unpredictable both the extent and the direction of changes in cholesterol levels in a given individual following a change in dietary cholesterol.

level, as would have been expected from the lipid hypothesis. Among those who observed a drop in their serum cholesterol, 21 out of 28 (75 per cent) experienced a drop which was less than 20 mg per 100 ml, or less than 10 per cent of the initial value. This great variation in response to a reduction in dietary cholesterol was observed in both men and women.

Variations of this kind render unpredictable the effect on serum cholesterol of a sudden change in dietary cholesterol. This phenomenon, observed by several authors[35-38] is recognized as of major importance by Ahrens[39] who questioned the soundness and desirability of recommendations aimed at reducing dietary cholesterol intake in the free-living population.

Many other important experiments were carried out with human subjects where the effect of dietary cholesterol on serum cholesterol levels was studied under well-controlled conditions. Most experiments, however, were carried out with subjects confined to institutions, such as prisons, mental hospitals, sometimes universities! Furthermore, the diets differed greatly from the normal North American diet. In such experiments, one could note a statistically significant effect on serum cholesterol associated with cholesterol intake. The results of these experiments were tabulated by McGill[20].

So as to obtain a valid comparison between several experiments, dietary cholesterol was expressed as milligrams of cholesterol per 1,000 kcal per day[20]. Assuming that a person consumes 2,500 kcal per day, cholesterol intake in a diet containing 150 mg of cholesterol per 1,000 calories, would be 375 mg per day; if the choice of food is such that the diet contains 300 mg of cholesterol per 1,000 kcal, that same person would consume 750 mg of cholesterol daily. This would probably be the range of cholesterol intake for most North Americans. Calculations show that a reduction in cholesterol intake from approximately 800 to 300 mg per day would be associated with a drop in the serum cholesterol level between zero per cent and 15 per cent. Great variations in the results obtained from one experiment to another were obvious[20].

In the experiments reported above, the subjects were, as described, inmates of various institutions. In such institutions, the diet of the experimental subjects was carefully controlled, and little opportunity was available for individuals to return to their usual food habits. These conditions do not reflect the usual conditions of the free-living population.

Would it not be important then to verify the response of free-living persons to a change in the intake of dietary cholesterol? Flynn and his colleagues[38] of the University of Missouri-Columbia reported interesting data in this respect. They carried out an experiment involving 116 male volunteers averaging 46 years of age. The experiment lasted six months; experimental design and data processing were in line with current biostatistical criteria. During the first three months, half of the subjects added two eggs daily to their regular diet whereas the other half maintained their usual diet without adding any egg. During the following three months, the diets were reversed: those who ate two additional eggs daily stopped taking these eggs and those who had kept their usual diet added two eggs as planned in the experimental protocol. The daily consumption of two eggs corresponded to an additional intake of 500 mg of cholesterol.

The results of that experiment are presented in Fig 34. Adding two eggs daily to or withdrawing them from the diet had no effect at all on

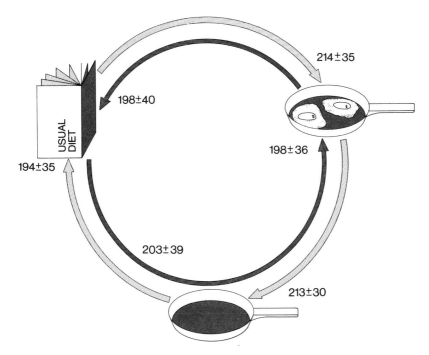

Fig. 34—The effect on serum cholesterol levels in men of adding and withdrawing two eggs (500 mg of cholesterol) daily to and from a usual diet.

(Adapted from Flynn *et al*[38].)

This figure illustrates the results of an experiment involving 116 healthy free-living men averaging 46 years of age. Adding two eggs daily, that is an equivalent of 500 mg of cholesterol, to the usual diet or withdrawing them had no effect whatever on serum cholesterol level. These additional observations supported the conclusions reached by many investigators that additional dietary cholesterol taken with the usual diet had practically no effect on serum cholesterol levels in free-living healthy individuals.

serum cholesterol levels. It is important to remember that the subjects involved in this particular experiment were free-living individuals who were consuming a diet typical of North Americans.

These observations, surprising as they may be within the context of a generalized phobia with regard to dietary cholesterol, merely confirmed the conclusions reached by Gertler, Garn and White[22] in 1950, Keys et al[21] in 1956, Morris et al[25] in 1963, Kahn et al[26] in 1969, Wen and Gershoff[19] in 1973, Slater et al[36] in 1976, Olivier[40] in 1976, Hodgson et al[27] in 1976, Kummerow et al[41] in 1977, Porter et al[42] in 1977, Truswell[37] in 1978, Ahrens[39] in 1979, and Grundy[43] in 1979.

In closing, let us repeat the question implied at the beginning of this chapter: Is there a correlation between the cholesterol taken with a regular diet and serum cholesterol level? We must conclude that:

The intake of dietary cholesterol has no significant effect on the concentration of cholesterol in the blood of healthy persons representative of the general population.

This point of view has been shared by Health and Welfare Canada[44] since 1977, and was unequivocally adopted by the United States Food and Nutrition Board, National Research Council[45].

This chapter, in retrospect, could have been titled: "Exoneration of dietary cholesterol as a risk factor for coronary heart disease". Let us hope that the data presented herein will help reassure the reader with respect to dietary cholesterol and relieve the neurosis which, in this regard, still haunts the North American consumer.

REFERENCES

1. Anitschkow NN: A history of experimentation on arterial atherosclerosis in animals. In Blumenthal HT (ed) *Cowdey's Arteriosclerosis: A Survey of the Problem* (ed 2), pp 21–44. Springfield, Thomas, 1967

2. Kannel WB, McGee D, Gordon T: A general cardiovascular risk profile: the Framingham Study. *Am J Cardiol,* 38:46–51, 1976

3. Carlson LA, Olsson AG: Serum-lipoprotein-cholesterol distribution in healthy men with high serum-cholesterol concentrations: extrapolation to clofibrate trial. *Lancet,* 1:869–870, 1979

4. Kannel WB: Some lessons in cardiovascular epidemiology from Framingham. *Am J Cardiol,* 37:269–282, 1976

5. Wright IS: Correct levels of serum cholesterol. Average vs normal vs optimal. *JAMA,* 236:261–262, 1976

6. Stamler J: Population studies. In Levy RI, Rifkind BM, Dennis BH, Ernst ND (eds) *Nutrition, Lipids, and Coronary Heart Disease. A Global View* p 57. New York, Raven Press, 1979

7. Reiser R: The three weak links in the diet-heart disease connection. *Nutrition Today,* 14:22–28, 1979

8. Carlson LA, Böttiger LE: Ischaemic heart-disease in relation to fasting values of plasma triglycerides and cholesterol. *Lancet,* 1:865–868, 1972

9. Keys A: Coronary heart disease in seven

countries. American Heart Association, Monograph 29. *Circulation*, 41: suppl 1, 1970

10. Tyroler HA, Heyden S, Bartel A, Cassel J, Cornoni JC, Hames, CG, Kleinbaum D: Blood pressure and cholesterol as coronary risk factors. *Arch Intern Med*, 128:907–914, 1971

11. Miller NE, Thelle DS, Førde OH, Mjøs OD: The Tromsø heart-study. High-density lipoprotein and coronary heart-disease: A prospective case-control study. *Lancet*, 1:965–970, 1977

12. Robertson TL, Kato H, Gordon T, Kagan A, Rhoads GG, Land CE, Worth RM, Belsky JL, Dock DS, Miyanishi M, Kawamoto S: Epidemiologic studies of coronary heart disease and stroke in Japanese men living in Japan, Hawaii and California. Coronary heart disease risk factors in Japan and Hawaii. *Am J Cardiol*, 39:244–249, 1977

13. McGee D, Gordon T: The Framingham Study—an epidemiological investigation of cardiovascular disease. Sect 31. The results of the Framingham Study applied to four other U.S.-based epidemiologic studies of cardiovascular disease, U.S. Department of Health, Education, and Welfare. Publication No (NIH) 76-1083. Washington, DC, DHEW, 1976

14. Levy RI, Rifkind BM, Dennis BH, Ernst ND: In Levy RI, Rifkind BM, Dennis BH, Ernst ND (eds) *Nutrition, Lipids, and Coronary Heart Disease. A Global View*. Nutrition in health and disease, vol 1. New York, Raven Press, 1979

15. Holme I, Helgeland A, Hjermann I, Leren P, Lund-Larsen PG: Four and two-thirds years incidence of coronary heart disease in middle-aged men: the Oslo study. *Am J Epidemiol*, 112:149–160, 1980

16. Ahrens EH Jr: The management of hyperlipidemias: whether, rather than how. *Ann Internal Med*, 85:87–93, 1976

17. Masironi R: Dietary factors and coronary heart disease. *Bull WHO*, 42:103–114, 1970

18. Armstrong BK, Mann JI, Adelstein AM, Eskin F: Commodity consumption and ischemic heart disease mortality, with special reference to dietary practices. *J Chronic Dis*, 28:455–469, 1975

19. Wen C-P, Gershoff SN: Changes in serum cholesterol and coronary heart disease mortality associated with changes in the postwar Japanese diet. *Am J Clin Nutr*, 26:616–619, 1973

20. McGill HC Jr: The relationship of dietary cholesterol to serum cholesterol concentration and to atherosclerosis in man. *Am J Clin Nutr*, 32:2664–2702, 1979

21. Keys A, Anderson JT, Mickelsen O, Adelson SF, Fidanza F: Diet and serum cholesterol in man: lack of effect of dietary cholesterol. *J Nutr*, 59:39–56, 1956

22. Gertler MM, Garn SM, White PD: Diet, serum cholesterol and coronary artery disease. *Circulation*, 2:696–704, 1950

23. Gillum HL, Morgan AF, Jerome DW: Nutritional status of the aging. IV. Serum cholesterol and diet. *J Nutr*, 55:449–468, 1955

24. Paul O, Lepper MH, Phelan WH, Dupertuis GW, MacMillan A, McKean H, Park H: A longitudinal study of coronary heart disease. *Circulation*, 28:20–31, 1963

25. Morris JN, Marr JW, Heady JA, Mills GL, Pilkington TRE: Diet and plasma cholesterol in 99 bank men. *Br Med J*, 1:571–576, 1963

26. Kahn HA, Medalie JH, Neufeld HN, Riss E, Balogh M, Groen JJ: Serum cholesterol: its distribution and association with dietary and other variables in a survey of 10,000 men. *Isr J Med Sci*, 5:1117–1127, 1969

27. Hodgson PA, Ellefson RD, Elveback LR, Harris LE, Nelson RA, Weidman WH: Comparison of serum cholesterol in children fed high, moderate, or low cholesterol milk diets during neonatal period. *Metabolism*, 25:739–746, 1976

28. Frank GC, Berenson GS, Webber LS: Dietary studies and the relationship of diet to cardiovascular disease risk

factor variables in 10-year-old children—The Bogalusa Heart Study. *Am J Clin Nutr*, 31:328–340, 1978

29. Kannel WB, Gordon T: The Framingham diet study: Diet and the regulations of serum cholesterol (Sect 24). Washington, D.C., DHEW, 1970

30. Mann GV: Current concepts. Diet-heart: End of an era. *N Engl J Med*, 297:644–650, 1977

31. Nichols AB, Ravenscroft C, Lamphieard DE, Ostrander LD Jr: Daily nutritional intake and serum lipid levels. The Tecumseh study. *Am J Clin Nutr*, 29:1384–1392, 1976

32. Garcia-Palmieri MR, Tillotson J, Cordero E, Costas R Jr, Sorlie P, Gordon T, Kannel WB, Colon AA: Nutrient intake and serum lipids in urban and rural Puerto Rican men. *Am J Clin Nutr*, 30:2092–2100, 1977

33. Yano K, Rhoads GG, Kagan A: Coffee, alcohol and risk of coronary heart disease among Japanese men living in Hawaii. *N Engl J Med*, 297:405–409, 1977

34. Moore MS, Guzman MA, Schilling PE, Strong JP: Dietary-atherosclerosis study on deceased persons. *J Am Diet Assoc*, 70:602–606, 1977

35. Bronsgeest-Schoute DC, Hermus RJJ, Dallinga-Thie GM, Hautvast JGAJ: Dependence of the effects of dietary cholesterol and experimental conditions on serum lipids in man. III. The effect on serum cholesterol of removal of eggs from the diet of free-living habitually egg-eating people. *Am J Clin Nutr*, 32:2193–2197, 1979

36. Slater G, Mead J, Dhopeshwarkar G, Robinsons S, Alfin-Slater RB: Plasma cholesterol and triglycerides in men with added eggs in the diet. *Nutr Rep Int*, 14:249–260, 1976

37. Truswell AS: Diet and plasma lipids—

a reappraisal. *Am J Clin Nutr*, 31:977–989, 1978

38. Flynn MA, Nolph GB, Flynn TC, Kahrs R, Krause G: Effect of dietary egg on human serum cholesterol and triglycerides. *Am J Clin Nutr*, 32:1051–1057, 1979

39. Ahrens EH: Dietary fats and coronary heart disease: unfinished business. *Lancet*, 2:1345–1348, 1979

40. Olivier M: Dietary cholesterol, plasma cholesterol and coronary heart disease. *Br Heart J*, 38:214–218, 1976

41. Kummerow FA, Kim Y, Hull Pollard J, Ilinou P, Dorossiev DL, Valek J: The influence of egg consumption on the serum cholesterol level in human subjects. *Am J Clin Nutr*, 30:664–673, 1977

42. Porter MW, Yamanaka W, Carlson SD, Flynn MA: Effect of dietary egg on serum cholesterol and triglyceride of human males. *Am J Clin Nutr*, 30:490–495, 1977

43. Grundy SM: Dietary fats and sterols. In Levy RI, Rifkind BM, Dennis BH, Ernst ND, (eds) *Nutrition, Lipids, and Coronary Heart Disease. A Global View*, pp 89–118. New York, Raven Press, 1979

44. Health and Welfare Canada: Recommendations for prevention programs in relation to nutrition and cardiovascular disease. Recommendations of the Committee on Diet and Cardiovascular Disease, as amended and adopted by Department of National Health and Welfare, June, 1977

45. United State Food and Nutrition Board. Toward Healthful Diets. Food and Nutrition Board, Division of Biological Sciences, Assembly of Life Sciences, National Research Council. Washington, D.C. *National Academy of Sciences*, 1980

5
Saturated and polyunsaturated fats

INTRODUCTION

Dietary fats consist of mixed triglycerides which are formed by the esterification of glycerol with saturated and unsaturated fatty acids (See Chapter 1). Fats are said to be saturated if they contain a sizable proportion of saturated fatty acids, as compared with unsaturated fats which are rich in unsaturated fatty acids. Fats of animal origin are generally considered to be saturated and fats of vegetable origin unsaturated. The two types of fat contain both saturated and unsaturated fatty acids but the ratios differ in each class.

Saturated fatty acids, as already explained, have saturated carbon chains, that is the carbon atoms are saturated with hydrogen; unsaturated fatty acids, on the other hand, have unsaturated carbon chains and lack hydrogen at specific points—the double bonds. Unsaturated fatty acids are either monounsaturated or polyunsaturated, the mono-unsaturated acids are those such as oleic acid (C18:1) which have only one double bond, and the polyunsaturated acids, for example, linoleic (C18:2ω6) and linolenic acids (C18:3ω3), are those which have two or more double bonds. Polyunsaturated fatty acids are often designated by the letters PUFA (Polyunsaturated Fatty Acids).

The nutritionists' interest in PUFA goes back to the 1950s when many investigators considered the possibility that the daily consumption of large amounts of vegetable fats rich in PUFA might help to lower blood cholesterol[1]. At that time, the lipid hypothesis discussed in the previous chapter, which is based on the suggested relationship between the serum cholesterol level and cardiovascular disease mortality, led to the belief that it would be beneficial to reduce blood cholesterol and that this could be done through the diet. This is why attention turned to the consumption of unsaturated fats and PUFA as a means of reducing blood cholesterol and thus preventing heart disease. It is therefore pertinent to review and analyze the scientific data that have been published on the subject in order to assess the relationship between PUFA intake and the incidence of cardiovascular disease.

COMPOSITION OF EDIBLE FATS AND OILS

Animal fats have a high percentage of saturated fatty acids with a chain length of 12–18 carbon atoms (Table 13). Butter, for example, contains about 50 per cent 12–18 carbon saturated fatty acids. It also contains about 10 per cent 4–10 carbon or short-chain fatty acids. This short-chain fatty acid content is specific for butter and is partly responsible for its physical properties (such as melting point) and for its pleasant taste. Beef and pork fats contain about 40 per cent or more of long-chain and medium-chain saturated fatty acids. The polyunsaturated fatty acid content of animal fats generally ranges from 4.0 to 30 per cent (Table 13).

Vegetable fats on the other hand, particularly corn, soybean and sunflower seed oils, contain less than 15 per cent long-chain saturated fatty acids and more than 55 per cent polyunsaturated fatty acids. It should be

TABLE 13

FATTY ACID CONTENT OF SOME DIETARY FATS
(g per 100 g of fat)*

Source of fat	C4:0– C10:0	Lauric (C12:0)	Myristic (C14:0)	Palmitic (C16:0)	Stearic (C18:0)	Oleic (C18:1)	PUFA[1]	P/S[2] Ratio
FATS OF ANIMAL ORIGIN								
Butter	8.7	2.8	10.1	26.3	12.1	25.1	3.7	0.09
Tallow	0.1	0.9	3.7	24.8	18.7	36.0	4.3	0.15
Lard	0.1	0.5	1.4	23.7	13.0	40.9	11.4	0.45
Poultry	0.2	1.0	1.2	23.8	6.4	39.2	17.6	0.68
Atlantic herring[3]	—	—	7.2	12.0	1.1	12.0	13.9	0.69
Menhadden	—	—	9.0	19.0	3.8	15.5	28.5	1.02
FATS OF VEGETABLE ORIGIN								
Coconut oil	14.1	43.7	16.4	8.2	3.0	5.7	1.8	0.03
Cocoa butter	—	—	0.1	25.4	33.2	32.6	3.0	0.12
Olive oil	—	—	—	11.5	2.3	71.5	8.9	0.78
Peanut oil	—	—	0.1	9.5	2.3	45.6	31.0	3.23
Canola oil	—	—	—	4.8	1.5	53.2	33.2	4.80
Soybean oil	—	0.1	0.2	10.7	3.9	22.8	57.6	5.28
Corn oil	—	—	—	10.7	1.7	24.6	58.1	5.43
Sunflower seed oil	—	—	0.1	5.8	4.1	21.7	66.7	11.31

* Data selected from Sheppard et al[2]
[1] Polyunsaturated = C18:2, C18:3, C20:2, etc
[2] Polyunsaturated/saturated ratio: based solely on lauric, myristic and palmitic acids[3] as saturated fatty acids (see Chapter 5)
[3] Contains 21.5 per cent erucic acid

noted however that all vegetable fats do not have a PUFA content as high as these three types of oil: for example olive oil and coconut fat contain less than 10 per cent PUFA.

EPIDEMIOLOGICAL STUDIES

In view of the saturated fatty acid content of fats of animal origin, a relationship has long been sought between mortality from coronary heart disease and the intake of animal fats. This possibility was investigated in many extensive epidemiological studies. Fig 35 is an example of the relationship observed between the consumption of foods of animal origin (eggs, meat, poultry and dairy products) and the mortality from coronary heart disease. The data of Fig 35 were taken from a study conducted in twenty countries.

In Fig 35 a straight line was drawn through the twenty points representing the data from these twenty countries which may lead to the conclusion that there is a correlation between mortality and the portion of calories provided by foods of animal origin. In fact the correlation coefficient of 0.725 in this case is highly significant from the statistical standpoint. Once again, one should note, however, that this correlation is purely mathematical in nature, and that it does not necessarily prove a cause-and-effect relationship. Yet the interpretation too often made by some investigators, the mass media and others is one of a cause-and-effect relationship.

The reader's attention has already been drawn to this kind of mathematical relationship and to the fallacious interpretation that can be put on it. Simple correlation studies are of little use when many factors, other than those related to nutrition, may influence the incidence of coronary heart disease. A closer examination of the data in Fig 35 shows that most points are clustered in one area of the curve and that it is questionable whether the original interpretation is valid. Any biostatistician would readily agree that under such conditions the mathematical relationship, although highly significant, is of little practical value. Indeed, most authors dealing with this kind of relationship are aware of its limitations but, unfortunately, the interpretation put on the data by the investigator is not always the same as that which eventually reaches the public at large. The animal industry has already experienced the consequences of such wrong interpretations of the scientific data[6]. Once again, those who work in the field of nutrition and public health are urged to be extremely cautious in their interpretation of this kind of mathematical association.

Several epidemiological studies have shown, in a similar fashion, a significant mathematical correlation between the serum cholesterol level in individuals and the consumption of saturated fatty acids, often calculated from statistical data. For example, the study in seven countries[7] showed, as all others, a highly significant correlation ($r = 0.89$) between these two

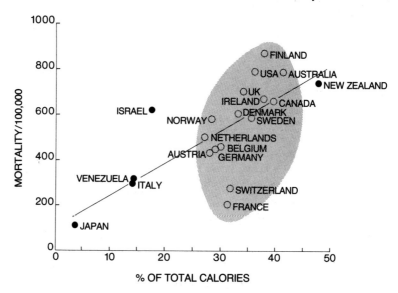

Fig. 35—Mathematical relationship between the percentage of calories introduced into the diet by foods of animal origin (eggs, meat, poultry and dairy products) and the incidence of mortality from coronary heart disease.

(Data selected and adapted from Stamler[4,5] using the 1973 CHD mortality rates for men.)

Animal fats are rich in saturated fatty acids. For this reason, a correlation has been sought between the intake of foods of animal origin (eggs, meat, poultry and dairy products) and the incidence of coronary heart disease. Data from the twenty-country study are shown in this figure. It can be seen that for 75 per cent of the countries under study there would be only a very small correlation between the two variables as indicated by the eliptical area which covers them. Unfortunately certain epidemiologists yielded to the temptation of seeing in these data a cause-and-effect relationship between calories provided by animal products and coronary heart disease. Once more it must be remembered that this figure illustrates what is no more than a mathematical relationship, and not at all a cause-and-effect relationship. Furthermore, it must be realized that the correlation is an extremely weak one on account of the variation observed from one country to another. The simple correlation illustrated in this figure is a method of investigation which is no longer used by biostatisticians and modern epidemiologists or, if they use it, they attach little significance thereto because many other factors related to nutrition and the incidence of coronary heart disease can influence the results. The reader is urged to appreciate the limitations of the type of relationship illustrated in this figure.

variables. A close examination of the data, however, reveals that, although the serum cholesterol level ranged from 160 to 260 mg per 100 ml, polyunsaturated fatty acids in all cases contributed about 4 per cent of total calories; this varied very little from one country to another. As a result, it is impossible to show any correlation between the consumption of polyunsaturated fatty acids and the serum cholesterol level. In a similar manner, it is impossible to demonstrate a beneficial role of PUFA as far as mortality from coronary heart disease is concerned[8]. Epidemiological studies like those just mentioned seem to suggest a positive mathematical correlation between the intake of saturated fatty acids and blood cholesterol[4,19]; but they suggest no relationship whatsoever between the intake of polyunsaturated fatty acids (PUFA) and blood cholesterol levels and, as a consequence, no link between the intake of PUFA and mortality from coronary heart disease.

CONTROLLED EXPERIMENTS

Since epidemiological studies such as those just described provide only hints as to possible relationships between different variables, it is desirable to carry out controlled experiments to define and measure the true relationships between variables of interest. In the present case, we want to know whether or not the mathematical relationship shown to exist can be correlated with a biological relationship, that is whether or not the nature of dietary fat has any effect on serum cholesterol and the incidence of coronary heart disease.

There is a large body of data tending to show that the replacement of dietary fats high in saturated fatty acids with fats high in PUFA results in a small lowering of serum cholesterol level in humans[1,3,9-16]. Keys and his collaborators[3] even suggested a mathematical formula aimed at predicting changes in serum cholesterol level according to changes in the intake of saturated fatty acids and PUFA. This formula can be written as follows:

$$\Delta Chol = 1.2 \, (2S' - P)$$

where

ΔChol	= the change expected in serum cholesterol level expressed as mg per 100 ml.
S'	= the change in the amount of saturated fatty acids expressed as a percentage of total calories.
P	= the change in the amount of PUFA also expressed as a percentage of total calories.

To arrive at this formula, Keys and his collaborators carried out several experiments and also used results obtained in other laboratories. They first showed that stearic acid (C18:0) is a saturated acid with little or no influence on blood cholesterol and suggested that this saturated fatty acid could be omitted when using the formula. The same probably holds for the readily metabolized short-chain saturated fatty acids (C4 to C10) which are important constituents of butter and coconut oil. The term S' in the above formula therefore may be applied only to C12, C14 and C16 saturated fatty acids namely, lauric, myristic and palmitic acids.

It is difficult to understand why stearic acid, a long-chain fatty acid, would have no effect on blood cholesterol when lauric, myristic and palmitic acids having shorter chain lengths would be active. Advocates and users of the Keys formula are always discomfited by this question. Lastly, it is interesting to note that if the Keys formula is applicable, 95 per cent of the saturated fatty acids found in beef and pork, 50 per cent of the saturated fatty acids found in butter and 20 per cent of the saturated fatty acids found in coconut oil must be without effect on the blood cholesterol level.

As far as polyunsaturated fatty acids are concerned, the Keys formula predicts that they should be quite ineffective in lowering the blood cholesterol level. In fact, as the formula indicates, one would have to consume 2 g of PUFA to offset the effect of 1 g of saturated fatty acids taken in the form of lauric, myristic and palmitic acids. In view of this inefficiency, one might question the recommendations aimed at increasing the intake of unsaturated fats if the objective is to lower blood cholesterol.

In this respect, let us examine some characteristics of the diets used in the derivation of the above formula. To our knowledge, in attempting to show the role of PUFA in cholesterolemia, the two diets used were such that in one, the high PUFA level was accompanied by a lower cholesterol level than in the low PUFA diet. Similarly, the high PUFA diet had a lower content of saturated fatty acids than the low PUFA diet. We are therefore left to solve two equations for three variables—a mathematical impossibility[17]. It is thus not surprising that there are many cases where Keys formula does not apply[7,12,16,18]. This is why Hegsted and his collaborators[12] suggested another formula which takes into account dietary cholesterol in addition to saturated fatty acids and PUFA. Investigators now have two formulae available[17]. It is interesting to observe how the available data always seems to fit the chosen formula.

In order to conclude that there is a beneficial effect from polyunsaturated fatty acids on blood cholesterol, it would be necessary to carry out tests in which the PUFA level in the diet is the sole variable under study. In the meantime, it must be realized that studies on the effect of PUFA on blood cholesterol have been confused by the possible effects of other variables which, to date, have not been controlled satisfactorily.

It would thus be a mistake to believe that the hypocholesterolemic effect of PUFA has been proved by rigorously controlled scientific experiments.

THE POLYUNSATURATED/SATURATED (P/S) RATIO

If the hypothesis were accepted that the intake of polyunsaturated fatty acids lowers serum cholesterol, one would also have to accept that a given dietary fat would be hypocholesterolemic only if its PUFA content were higher than its lauric (C12:0), myristic (C14:0) and palmitic (C16:0) acid content by a factor greater than two. This explains why the ratio between the concentration of polyunsaturated fatty acids and that of saturated fatty acids is sometimes used to characterize dietary fats. This ratio is commonly designated by the symbol P/S. A P/S ratio lower than 1.0 is characteristic of a fat with a saturated fatty acid content greater than that of its polyunsaturated fatty acids. A P/S ratio greater than 1.0 indicates a fat higher in PUFA than in saturated fatty acids.

As lauric (C12:0), myristic (C14:0) and palmitic (C16:0) acids are the saturated fatty acids considered in Keys formula, the P/S ratio of different dietary fats can be calculated on the basis of these acids only. Table 13 gives the P/S ratio of some fats and oils calculated with their respective PUFA contents as the numerator and the sum of lauric, myristic and palmitic acid contents as the denominator. The P/S ratio of animal fats is always among the lowest and that of corn, soybean and sunflower seed oils among the highest. In this respect, however, let us note that certain oils of vegetable origin have a lower P/S ratio than fats of animal origin. The P/S ratio could thus be used as an index of the degree of saturation or unsaturation of dietary fats. It could also be used as an index of the polyunsaturated fatty acid content of given diets.

As mentioned earlier, there are several studies indicating that the substitution in the diet of low P/S ratio saturated fats by high P/S ratio high PUFA fats would result in a lowering of the serum cholesterol level. It was thought desirable, however, to examine in practical terms the extent of this postulated hypocholesterolemic effect, and the most representative and frequently mentioned experiments in the scientific literature were studied. Let us note first that the usual edible oils rich in PUFA contain no cholesterol while saturated fats generally contain cholesterol in varying quantities. It is very difficult to formulate diets where the P/S ratio is the sole variable.

In one experiment, to circumvent this difficulty, the normal fatty acid composition of pig and beef body fats was changed by modifying the fat portion of the ration. By so doing, fats of animal origin could be produced with a high PUFA content and, as a result, diets for human subjects could be formulated with different saturated/unsaturated fat ratios, and a cholesterol level roughly identical in all cases. Under these conditions, it has been possible to raise the P/S ratio for beef fat from 0.09 to 0.89, a rise of nearly 1,000 per cent, and the P/S ratio for pork fat from 0.46 to 2.00, an increase of 435 per cent. When these fats were incorporated in the diets, in both cases, serum cholesterol dropped in experimental subjects by a factor of only about 7.5 per cent (Table 14). This drop, significant as it may be from the biostatistical standpoint, may be of no biological significance from a practical point of view.

Another example of the negligible effect of polyunsaturated fatty acids on blood cholesterol can be seen in data reported by the American Heart Association. On the recommendation of this Association, a particular diet was tested for six months in men aged 21–60. At the beginning of the experiment the subjects had a mean serum cholesterol level of 233 mg per 100 ml. Fig 36 shows certain characteristics of this diet and the results obtained[20].

As the experiment progressed, the serum cholesterol level decreased by 9–10 per cent, compared with the initial value observed when the men were consuming a pre-experimental control diet. Scrutinizing some characteristics of the test diet, however, it can be seen that the effect of

TABLE 14

COMPARATIVE EFFECTS OF SATURATED AND UNSATURATED FATS INCORPORATED INTO THE DIET ON THE SERUM CHOLESTEROL LEVEL IN MAN*

Fats	Saturated fatty acids: C14:0 + C16:0 (%)	Linoleic acid C18:2ω6 (%)	P/S ratio	Serum cholesterol (mg/100 ml)	Change (Δ %)
		BEEF FAT			
Saturated	36	0.3	0.09	211	
Unsaturated	25	23	0.89	195	−7.5
		PORK FAT			
Saturated	26	12	0.46	185	
Unsaturated	18	36	2.00	171	−7.4

* Based on Nestel et al[10,11]

The composition of pork fat may be modified by changing the fatty acid composition of the fat portion of the ration. In ruminants, fats added to the ration must be coated to protect them against the action of the microorganisms in the rumen. In this way, it is possible to obtain animal fats that are rich in polyunsaturated fatty acids. This table shows the effect of such modified animal fats on serum cholesterol in subjects consuming 45–50 per cent of their total calories in the form of fat. In this particular case, the P/S ratio increased by a factor of 1,000 per cent in beef fat and 435 per cent in pork. With both modified fats serum cholesterol dropped by a factor of only about 7.5 per cent. The P/S ratio of dietary fats, therefore, seems to have little influence on serum cholesterol levels in man.

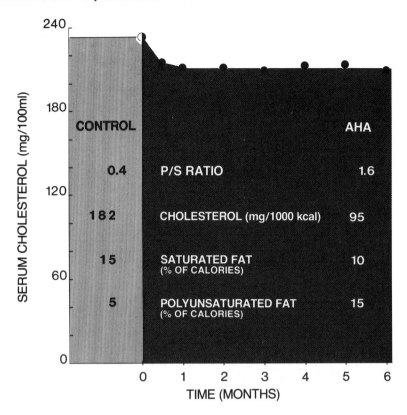

Fig. 36—Effect of the American Heart Association diet on blood cholesterol in men aged 21–60 years.

(Data selected and adapted from Wilson *et al*[20].)

This figure shows that major changes in the composition of the diet have little effect on the serum cholesterol level in men aged 21–60 years. Note that the American Heart Association diet, in addition to having a PUFA content three times as high as the control diet, also contains half as much cholesterol. Under such conditions, it is impossible to discriminate between the effect of PUFA intake and that of dietary cholesterol. The slight drop in serum cholesterol could thus be explained by the fall in the intake of dietary cholesterol as well as by the rise in the intake of PUFA. When two variables are thus confounded, it is impossible to distinguish on a scientific basis the effects of one variable from that of the other. An interpretation favoring solely the PUFA intake would thus be misleading.

polyunsaturated fatty acids was confused with the effect of dietary cholesterol. The Association's diet contained more PUFA than the control diet
but at the same time only half as much cholesterol. The slight drop in blood
cholesterol observed in this test could thus have been caused, at least in
part, by the drop in dietary cholesterol[12,21]. Under such conditions, it
becomes impossible to distinguish between the effect due to the intake of
PUFA and that of a reduction in dietary cholesterol. An interpretation
favoring solely the PUFA intake would be misleading. In any case, the
hypocholesterolemic effect associated with the replacement of saturated
fats by fats high in PUFA had little effect from a practical point of view.

There is another large-scale experiment often referred to in the literature dealing with the effect of saturated vs unsaturated fats on blood
cholesterol, namely the National Diet-Heart Study. This study included
1,000 men aged 40–59 years, known to be healthy and having no history
of heart disease. The results of this study and some characteristics of the
diets tested are shown in Fig 37.

In the National Diet Heart study, the cholesterol levels of the two
diets tested do not vary by more than 10 per cent, whereas the P/S ratios
differ by 400 percent. In this case, since the type of fat used in both diets
was of animal origin, we might consider that the effect of the nature of the
dietary fatty acids on serum cholesterol was not confounded with that of
dietary cholesterol.

Unfortunately, here again, it is impossible to differentiate between the
effect of a low intake of saturated fatty acids and a high intake of PUFA
because both types of fatty acids vary in opposite directions in both diets.
Nevertheless, the high PUFA, low saturated fatty acid diet, as compared
to the control diet, induced a drop of about 9 per cent in serum cholesterol
which lasted throughout the whole experiment of 52 weeks. Despite this
clear-cut response, a question remains as to the true meaning of such a
small drop in serum cholesterol with regard to the development of atherosclerosis and the prevention of coronary heart disease in the public at
large.

Changing the P/S ratio of the diet from 0.4 to 1.6, as was the case in
this experiment, requires drastic changes in food habits. As a matter of
fact, to adopt diets high in polyunsaturated fatty acids (PUFA) with a P/S
ratio of 1.6 or more, in terms of day-to-day life, would mean for the vast
majority of North-Americans the acceptance of a dull, tasteless and unattractive diet. As stated by Oster[22], there is no population known to
consume a diet in which PUFA provide as many calories as the diet used
in the National Heart Study. A partial proof of this is the study in seven
countries[7] where PUFA supplied only 4–5 per cent of total calories in the
normal diet of strikingly different populations. Changing one's customary
diet for one similar to that used in the National Heart Study and obtaining
so little effect on blood cholesterol would be of little interest for the pop-

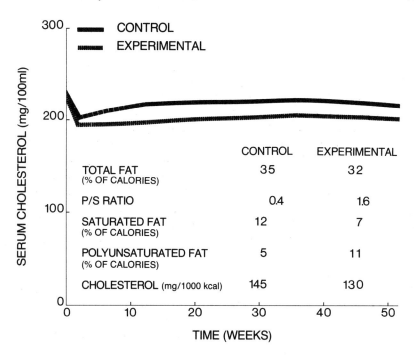

	CONTROL	EXPERIMENTAL
TOTAL FAT (% OF CALORIES)	35	32
P/S RATIO	0.4	1.6
SATURATED FAT (% OF CALORIES)	12	7
POLYUNSATURATED FAT (% OF CALORIES)	5	11
CHOLESTEROL (mg/1000 kcal)	145	130

Fig. 37—Changes in serum cholesterol level following a drastic change in food habits.

(Based on data reported by the National Diet-Heart Study Research Group[16].)

The National Diet-Heart Study was a large-scale experiment often referred to in order to show the effect on blood cholesterol of a change in certain food habits. This is one of the few studies where cholesterol intake was almost the same in each of the diets tested. Under the conditions of this experiment, a simultaneous decrease in saturated fatty acids and an increase in PUFA intake induced a drop in serum cholesterol by a factor of only about 9 per cent. It appears that such a drastic change in diet with such a little effect on serum cholesterol would be of little interest for the population at large, especially in view of the fact that the very significance of the relationship between serum cholesterol and coronary heart disease is still unresolved.

ulation at large. This is especially true in view of the fact that the importance of blood cholesterol in the development of coronary disease is seriously questioned in scientific and medical circles.

The Tecumseh Study, the results of which were published recently[18], also deals with the effect of diet on blood lipids and serum cholesterol in particular. This study was carried out in Tecumseh, Michigan, and involved 2,000 men and women between the ages of 16 and 69. Each subject's intake of saturated animal fats, unsaturated vegetable fats, cholesterol, and other components was evaluated.

The subjects, after correction for age and sex, were divided into three groups (tertiles) according to their blood cholesterol level. The first group (tertile) consisted of persons with the lowest blood cholesterol concentration, the second was intermediate and the third the highest. The results in Fig 38 show that the different blood cholesterol levels were maintained from the lowest to the highest group (tertile) while the intake of saturated fats, of unsaturated fats and the P/S ratio of fats in the diet was the same

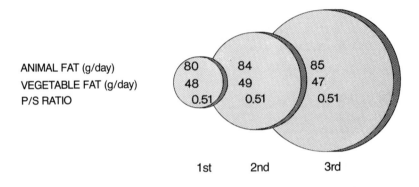

ANIMAL FAT (g/day)   80   84   85
VEGETABLE FAT (g/day)   48   49   47
P/S RATIO   0.51   0.51   0.51

              1st   2nd   3rd

SERUM CHOLESTEROL LEVELS GROUPED BY TERTILES

Fig. 38—Tertiles of serum cholesterol level in men and women taking part in the Tecumseh Study.

(From data published by Nichols et al[18].)

In a study carried out at Tecumseh, Michigan, 2,000 men and women aged 16–69 were grouped in tertiles according to their serum cholesterol levels. The first tertile consisted of those who had the lowest, the second, the intermediate and the third, the highest level. It was found that serum cholesterol levels varied from the lowest tertile to the highest even if the proportions of saturated and polyunsaturated fats and the P/S ratio remained constant. In other words the serum cholesterol level bore no relation to the type of fats consumed in the diet. The conclusion is that the serum cholesterol level is as independent of the type of fats taken in the diet as it is from their P/S ratio. This experiment provided additional support to the idea that the nature of dietary fat and the P/S ratio are of little importance in determining serum cholesterol levels in the general public.

for the three groups. In other words, the blood cholesterol level stayed higher or lower from one group to another even if the composition of the diet was the same. This gives additional support to the idea that the nature of dietary fats and the P/S ratio are of little importance in determining serum cholesterol levels in the general public.

In spite of all the experimental data casting much doubt on the real significance of the effect of polyunsaturated fatty acids on serum cholesterol levels, certain investigators advanced various hypotheses to explain how PUFA could bring about a drop in blood cholesterol. For example, it was claimed that polyunsaturated fatty acids could, in some cases, increase the fecal excretion of dietary cholesterol[17]. It was also believed that PUFA could cause a redistribution of cholesterol in body tissues other than blood[17]. The fall in blood cholesterol in this particular case could be considered as an artifact since the total amount of cholesterol in the body would remain the same. Even though these hypotheses appear plausible, they do not fully satisfy all scientific investigators[17].

The puzzle is greater still when saturated fatty acids are considered. In fact, nobody can explain, even in part, how the saturated fatty acids of butter, lard and tallow, for example, could really cause a rise in blood cholesterol. In order to do so, one would have to explain why the animal organism is normally synthesizing saturated fats when fed a fat-free diet. Furthermore, one would also have to explain why the absorption of dietary lipids, the deposition of adipose tissue and the anabolism of endogenous triglycerides do indeed favor saturated fatty acids as compared to PUFA.

It is well known, for example, that the triglycerides of chylomicrons are more saturated than those consumed if dietary fats are highly unsaturated. The biochemical processes taking place in the intestinal mucosa prevent an excessive degree of unsaturation in lipids entering the lymph circulation. It is also well known that lipids synthesized in the body from nutrients supplied by the diet are almost totally devoid of polyunsaturated fatty acids. It appears that the body tends to avoid the accumulation of PUFA rather than to store them. Before an increased consumption of polyunsaturated fatty acids is accepted as beneficial to human health, a satisfactory explanation should take these phenomena into account.

The fact that the animal body tends to protect itself against an accumulation of polyunsaturated fatty acids is not really surprising. It is known, in fact, that polyunsaturated fatty acids, such as linoleic acid (C18:2ω6), easily undergo peroxidation giving rise to free radicals, hydroperoxides, endoperoxides and other products. All these peroxidation products could cause serious damage at the cellular level[23] were they not controlled by the body. Under normal conditions, the cells are protected against these harmful peroxidation compounds by natural antioxidants such as vitamin E. This explains why an increased dietary intake of PUFA also increases the need for tocopherol (vitamin E).

Peroxidation reactions at the cellular level result in the formation of a wide variety of products including pigments of the lipofuscin type. While the chemistry of these compounds suggests that they are by-products of the peroxidation of polyunsaturated fatty acids, they are among the most indestructible substances, the least degradable and the most insoluble to accumulate in certain tissues of the body. Further, these products, like cholesterol, are found in atherosclerotic plaques and may contribute to the development and irreversibility of arterial lesions[24].

Another point of great concern is the damage that may be caused to biomembranes and the intracellular organelles by the peroxidation products of linoleic acid and other polyunsaturated fatty acids. The nature of this damage may be quite varied, as suggested by experiments carried out in the laboratory[22]. Mitochondria, microsomes and erythrocyte membranes are particularly sensitive to the peroxidation products of polyunsaturated fatty acids. It appears that certain free radicals formed during peroxidation reactions affect some cellular enzymes altering their normal activity. As a result abnormal products are formed and damage the cell[23].

Among the risks that might be associated with an increased consumption of linoleic acid and other polyunsaturated fatty acids, one should mention the risk of developing certain types of tumor. Carroll showed that the incidence of mammary tumors was 42 per cent higher in mice fed vegetable fats high in PUFA compared to mice fed animal fats[25-27]. Such data, of course, cannot be directly extrapolated to humans, but they emphasize the need for caution before recommending an increase in the consumption of linoleic acid and other polyunsaturated fatty acids.

Already some physicians caution against an increased consumption of polyunsaturated fatty acids[28]. For instance, it has been reported that increasing the intake of polyunsaturated fatty acids to supply 10 per cent of total calories might induce early ageing of cells, skin cells in particular[28]. A warning against the potential toxicity of linoleic acid and other PUFA appears in some publications[28,29], primarily because of the dangers associated with the peroxidation products of polyunsaturated fatty acids.

What would really be the extent of the danger if the consumption of fats high in PUFA were increased? Some will say that the risks would be low, especially if intake of vitamin E was also increased. Others would recommend caution pending more information on this subject.

Ahrens[30] seems to join the latter group as he lists no less than ten important points that should be clarified before we could safely recommend changes in food habits for the population at large. These ten points were inspired by the indisputable fact that the nature of dietary fats greatly influences the fatty acid composition of adipose tissue, phospholipids, cardiolipids, lipoproteins and cell membranes. Of the ten points raised, many concern the hazards associated with an increased consumption of linoleic acid ($C18:2\omega6$) and other polyunsaturated fatty acids.

In view of the information already given, the following questions would seem in order.

Could an increased consumption of linoleic acid and other PUFA affect the permeability of cellular membranes to materials such as drugs, foreign bodies, bacteria or viruses?

Could an increased consumption of linoleic acid and other PUFA bring about the early ageing of certain types of cells, particularly skin cells?

Could an increased consumption of linoleic acid and other PUFA bring about an imbalance between the different prostaglandins which play a role in blood coagulation?

Could an increased consumption of linoleic acid and other PUFA increase the risk of breast cancer?

Could an increased consumption of linoleic acid and other PUFA bring about modifications in cell receptors due to changes in the degree of saturation of membrane lipids? And, if so, what would be the consequences for the metabolism of lipoproteins?

In summary, all these uncertainties about the risks associated with an increased consumption of linoleic acid and other polyunsaturated fatty acids can only lead one to doubt the advisibility of any recommendation aimed at reducing the consumption of saturated fats and increasing that of polyunsaturated fats and oils. As seen earlier, dietary fat with a P/S ratio of 1.6 brings about little change in the serum cholesterol level. In a diet where the P/S ratio is 1.6, polyunsaturated fatty acids represent 10 per cent or more of total calories. Such a diet is dull, tasteless and unpalatable for North-Americans. Furthermore, there are no populations known to consume a diet with such a high PUFA level. In general, PUFA provide only 4–5 per cent of total calories, an amount sufficient to meet the requirements for essential fatty acids.

* Considering the slight effect that a diet high in linoleic acid and other polyunsaturated fatty acids has on serum cholesterol level, and
* considering the uncertainties relating to the dangers of an increased consumption of PUFA

it would seem that, for the moment, everyone concerned should be warned against all propaganda encouraging the general public to increase its consumption of linoleic acid and other polyunsaturated fatty acids.

REFERENCES

1. Ahrens EH Jr, Insull W Jr, Blomstrand R, Hirsch J, Tsaltas TT, Peterson ML: The influence of dietary fats on serum-lipid levels in man. *Lancet*, 1:943–953, 1957

2. Sheppard AJ, Iverson JL, Weihrauch

JL: Composition of selected dietary fats, oils, margarines, and butter. In Kuksis A (ed) *Handbook of Lipid Research.* vol 1, Fatty Acids and Glycerides, pp 341–379. New York, Plenum Press, 1978

3. Keys A, Anderson JT, Grande F: Serum cholesterol response to changes in the diet. IV. Particular saturated fatty acids in the diet. *Metabolism,* 14:776–787, 1965

4. Stamler J: Population studies. In Levy RI, Rifkind BM, Dennis BH, Ernst ND (eds) *Nutrition, Lipids, and Coronary Heart Disease. A Global View,* pp 25–88. New York, Raven Press, 1979

5. Stamler J: Research related to risk factors. *Circulation,* 60:1575–1587, 1979

6. Lofgren PA, Speckmann EW: Our industry today. Importance of animal products in the human diet. *J Dairy Sci,* 62:1019–1025, 1979

7. Keys A: Coronary heart disease in seven countries. American Heart Association, Monograph 29. *Circulation,* 41: suppl 1, 1970

8. Blackburn H: Coronary disease prevention. Controversy and professional attitudes. *Adv Cardiol,* 20:10–26, 1977

9. Keys A, Anderson JT, Grande F: Serum cholesterol response to changes in the diet. I. Iodine value of dietary fat versus 2S-P. *Metabolism,* 14:747–758, 1965

10. Nestel PJ, Havenstein N, Whyte HM, Scott TJ, Cook LJ: Lowering of plasma cholesterol and enhanced sterol excretion with the consumption of polyunsaturated ruminant fats. *N Engl J Med,* 288:379–382, 1973

11. Nestel PJ, Homma Y, Scott TW, Cook LJ, Havenstein N: Effect of dietary polyunsaturated pork on plasma lipids and sterol excretion in man. *Lipids,* 11:42–48, 1976

12. Hegsted DM, McGandy RB, Myers ML, Stare FJ: Quantitative effects of dietary fat on serum cholesterol in man. *Am J Clin Nutr,* 17:281–295, 1965

13. McGandy RB, Hegsted DM, Myers ML: Use of semisynthetic fats in determining effects of specific dietary fatty acids on serum lipids in man. *Am J Clin Nutr,* 23:1288–1298, 1970

14. Gattereau A, Delisle HF: The unsettled question: butter or margarine? *Can Med Assoc J,* 103:268–271, 1970

15. Anderson JT, Grande F, Keys A: Independence of the effects of cholesterol and degree of saturation of the fat in the diet on serum cholesterol in man. *Am J Clin Nutr,* 29:1184–1189, 1976

16. National Diet-Heart Study Research Group. National Diet-Heart Study final report. *Circulation,* 37,38: suppl 1, 1968

17. Jackson, RL, Taunton OD, Morrisett JD, Gotto AM: The role of dietary polyunsaturated fat in lowering blood cholesterol in man. *Circ Res,* 42:447–453, 1978

18. Nichols AB, Ravenscroft C, Lamphieard, DE, Ostrander LD Jr: Daily nutritional intake and serum lipid levels. The Tecumseh study. *Am J Clin Nutr,* 29:1384–1392, 1976

19. Stamler J, Lilienfeld, AM: Primary prevention of the atherosclerotic diseases. Atherosclerosis Study Group. Epidemiology Study Group. *Circulation,* 42:A-55–A-95, 1970

20. Wilson WS, Hulley SB, Burrows MI, Nichaman MZ: Serial lipid and lipoprotein responses to the American Heart Association fat-controlled diet. *Am J Med,* 51:491–503, 1971

21. Mattson FH, Erickson BA, Kligman AM: Effect of dietary cholesterol on serum cholesterol in man. *Am J Clin Nutr,* 25:589–594, 1972

22. Oster KA: Duplicity in a committee report on diet and coronary heart disease. *Am Heart J,* 99:409–412, 1980

23. Tappel AL: Lipid peroxidation damage to cell components. *Fed Proc,* 32:1870–1874, 1973

24. Jones RJ: Role of dietary fat in health. *J Am Oil Chem Soc,* 51:251–254, 1974

25. Carroll KK: Essential fatty acids: what level in the diet is most desirable? *Adv Exp Med Biol,* 83:535–546, 1977

26. Carroll KK, Khor HT: Effects of level and type of dietary fat on incidence of mammary tumors induced in female

Sprague-Dawley rats by 7,12-dimeth-ylbenz(α)anthracene. *Lipids,* 6:415–420, 1971

27. Carroll KK, Gammal EB, Plunkett ER: Hypothesis. Dietary fat and mammary cancer. *Can Med Assoc J,* 98:590–594, 1968

28. Pinckney ER: The potential toxicity of excessive polyunsaturates. *Am Heart J,* 85:723–726, 1973

29. Winkler HH, Frame B, Saeed SM, Spindler AC, Brouillette JN: Ceroid storage disease, complicated by rupture of the spleen. *Am J Med,* 46:297–301, 1969

30. Ahrens EH: Dietary fats and coronary heart disease: unfinished business. *Lancet,* 2:1345–1348, 1979

6
Lipoproteins

INTRODUCTION

Lipoproteins are blood-soluble, complex aggregates of proteins and lipids. They are the major carriers of cholesterol, cholesterol esters, phospholipids, triglycerides, and other lipids such as fat-soluble vitamins*. Lipoproteins are classified according to their density (weight/volume) into chylomicrons, VLDL (Very Low Density Lipoproteins), IDL (Intermediate Density Lipoproteins), LDL (Low Density Lipoproteins) and VHDL (Very High Density Lipoproteins). Chylomicrons are often excluded from the lipoprotein classification, despite having many characteristics in common with the other lipoproteins.

The VLDL are the largest but the lightest of the lipoproteins whereas HDL are the smallest but the heaviest. The VLDL contain the largest amount of triglycerides, the LDL the largest amount of cholesterol, and the HDL the largest amount of phospholipids and intermediate amounts of cholesterol.

In recent years, there has been an increasing interest in lipoproteins because of their role in human physiology. For example, LDL carry cholesterol to all body cells to ensure a steady supply of this compound which is essential for their normal functions. The role of HDL is not well known, but according to recent studies they might be involved in the prevention of atherosclerosis and ischemic heart disease. We shall therefore review the information available on the synthesis of lipoproteins as well as their main important physiological functions including their possible role in the development of cardiovascular disease. We shall also review the literature dealing with dietary and other factors thought to influence the concentration of the various types of lipoproteins in the blood.

_____

* See Chapter 1.

SYNTHESIS OF LIPOPROTEINS

Lipids found in the blood may be of exogenous or endogenous origin. Exogenous lipids originate from the diet while endogenous lipids are synthesized within the body by the liver and other organs. Because of this, fatty acids, triglycerides, phospholipids and cholesterol circulating in blood may come from the diet, but the metabolic activity of the intestinal mucosa, liver, adipose tissue and other organs may modify them rapidly, and sometimes extensively, after absorption.

The composition of the lipoproteins in blood is thus the result of many anabolic and catabolic reactions taking place within the body. These reactions are so complex and, in many cases, so difficult to measure quantitatively that we do not intend to distinguish in this book between exogenous and endogenous lipids. Our remarks will apply to the different classes of lipoproteins without attempting to explain the influence of their origin on the chemical composition of their component lipids.

Chylomicrons

Chylomicrons, like lipoproteins, are protein-lipid aggregates. It would appear logical to consider them as true lipoproteins. Chylomicrons are formed in the intestinal mucosa from absorbed dietary lipids and products of the anabolic and catabolic activity of the intestine. Before absorption, the dietary triglycerides are partially hydrolyzed in the intestinal lumen and then form aggregates with free fatty acids, cholesterol and bile salts; these aggregates are called micelles and carry the digested dietary fats to the villi where they are absorbed.

The mechanisms by which the micelles transfer their contents to the intestinal mucosa are still not well understood. It is known, however, that the cells of the intestinal mucosa have the ability to synthesize new triglycerides either from intact dietary fatty acids or from dietary fatty acids altered in their length or degree of saturation by the activity of the intestinal mucosa.

The intestinal mucosa is thus the first site where the body can affect the nature of ingested fats. The result of this metabolic activity is the production of fats more saturated than the original dietary fats if these are of vegetable origin, and less saturated if they are of animal origin. The intestinal mucosa, therefore, can saturate fatty acids derived from dietary fats high in polyunsaturated fatty acids, and can desaturate them when the dietary fats are rich in saturated fatty acids, as most animal fats are.

The triglycerides (TG) synthesized in the intestinal mucosa are then incorporated into the chylomicrons which also contain phospholipids (PL), esterified cholesterol (EC), free cholesterol (FC) and apolipoproteins of types A and B (see Apolipoproteins in Chapter 1). These chylomicrons then leave the intestinal mucosa, enter the lymph circulation and are discharged into the peripheral blood circulation at the level of the left subclavian vein.

The chylomicrons, enriched with Apo C following exchanges with HDL in the blood, are transported to the extrahepatic tissues where they yield their triglycerides (Fig 39). In these extrahepatic tissues, the lipoprotein lipase (LPL) accelerates the hydrolysis of triglycerides (TG). Fatty acids and diglycerides resulting from this hydrolysis are incorporated into the different tissues and are used as the need arises. The freed fatty acids for example may be used immediately as a source of cellular energy or may be resynthesized into triglycerides to be stored for future use.

Note that the activity of the enzyme lipoprotein lipase (LPL) is stimulated by the Apo C found at the surface of chylomicrons. This phenomenon explains why the clarification of blood serum, following the ingestion of fats, is rapidly effected in normal subjects. The half-life of chylomicrons in blood is approximately one hour only.

As the chylomicrons deliver their triglyceride content to the tissues, they become smaller, exchange Apo C with blood HDL and progressively form what is known as the "remnants". The remnants are rich in cholesterol and are ultimately degraded in the liver (Fig 39). The main function of the newly formed chylomicrons in the intestinal mucosa is therefore to transport the absorbed triglycerides, mainly of dietary origin, to the tissues where they become an immediate source of energy or are stored for future use.

Very Low Density Lipoproteins (VLDL)

The Very Low Density Lipoproteins are rich in triglycerides of endogenous origin and are synthesized in the liver. In addition, the liver synthesizes free cholesterol, cholesterol esters, phospholipids Apo B, Apo C and Apo E which are incorporated into VLDL (Fig 40).

Once they enter the blood circulation, the nascent VLDL are enriched with cholesterol esters through a reaction controlled by the enzyme, lecithin-cholesterol-acyl-transferase (LCAT), which has been of considerable interest during the past few years.

Lecithin-cholesterol-acyl-transferase (LCAT) is the main enzyme catalyzing the transfer of fatty acids found in the β position of phospholipids to free cholesterol. This enzyme is specific for the β position on the phospholipids. This means that the nature of the fatty acids found at this position determines the nature and solubility of the cholesterol esters formed in this way.

The free cholesterol taking part in this reaction is located at the surface of newly formed VLDL and lecithin-cholesterol-acyl-transferase (LCAT) is believed to be synthesized mainly in the liver. Furthermore the esteri-

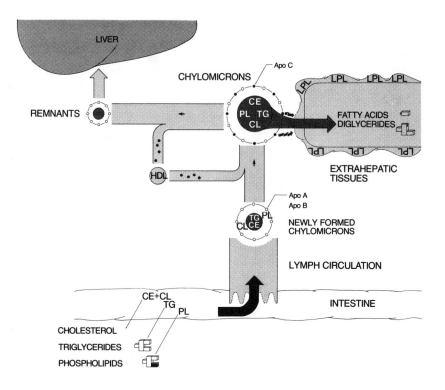

Fig. 39—Origin and fate of chylomicrons in the body.

(Based on references[1-6].)

Chylomicrons are formed in the intestinal mucosa from absorbed dietary lipids and products of the anabolic and catabolic activity in the mucosal cells. From there they enter into the lymph circulation to be discharged ultimately into the peripheral blood via the left subclavian vein. Enriched with Apo C through exchanges with blood HDL, the chylomicrons deliver their contents into extrahepatic tissues. The enzyme lipoprotein lipase (LPL) accelerates the process. Free fatty acids and diglycerides penetrate into the tissues concerned and may become an immediate source of energy or may be resynthesized in the form of triglycerides (TG). They may be deposited in tissues for future use.

As TG are delivered to the tissues, the chylomicrons become smaller, exchange Apo C with HDL, concentrate cholesterol and finally become what is known as the "remnants". The main function of the newly formed chylomicrons in the intestinal mucosa is to carry the absorbed triglycerides, mainly of dietary origin, to the tissues where they become an immediate source of cellular energy or are deposited in the adipose tissue for future use.

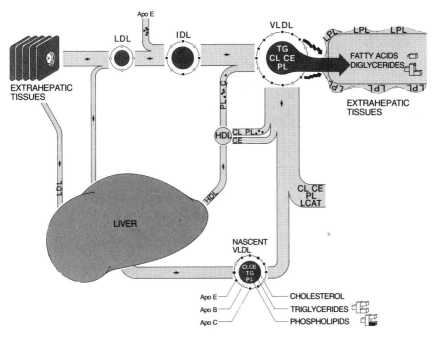

Fig. 40—*Origin and formation of VLDL, IDL and LDL.*

(Based on references[1-6].)

VLDL: This diagram shows that VLDL originate in the liver and are charged with endogenous triglycerides (TG) also synthesized in the liver. In blood they are enriched with cholesterol esters through the action of lecithin-cholesterol-acyl-transferase (LCAT). The VLDL then carry their contents to the extrahepatic tissues where they deliver their triglycerides and where they may become an immediate source of energy or be stored for future use.

LDL: LDL could be considered as the end-products following the progressive degradation of VLDL; IDL are intermediate products. During this degradation process the lipoprotein particles lose the major part of their triglycerides, but acquire additional quantities of free and esterified cholesterol, phospholipids and apolipoproteins. At the same time, their density increases and they become the lipoproteins classified as LDL.

fication of cholesterol through this reaction is greatly accelerated by the presence of Apo A supplied by HDL. Both VLDL and LDL acquire their cholesterol ester through this reaction. VLDL also increase their cholesterol ester content through exchanges with HDL and VLDL[3].

It could be concluded that VLDL are the main carriers of endogenous triglycerides from the liver where they are synthesized, to the tissues where they are utilized. At the tissue level they leave the blood through the action of lipoprotein lipase (LPL), and may become an immediate source of cellular energy or be stored for future use.

Low Density Lipoproteins (LDL)

It is difficult to distinguish between the VLDL and the LDL from the standpoint of their origin. In fact, the LDL could be considered as the end product of the various transformations undergone by the VLDL (Fig 40). As the VLDL deliver their triglycerides to the body tissues, they gradually concentrate the free and esterified cholesterol, the phospholipids and the apolipoproteins. The loss of triglycerides is accompanied by a decrease in their volume and an accumulation of cholesterol, cholesterol esters, phospholipids and apolipoproteins.

The increased concentration of cholesterol esters in LDL is obviously linked to the action of lecithin-cholesterol-acyl-transferase (LCAT), as described above (Fig 40), and to exchanges with HDL. During this process, the apolipoproteins, other than Apo B, gradually leave VLDL and move in part towards HLD. When the major part of the triglycerides in the original VLDL has been delivered to the tissues and when the concentration of cholesterol esters in the changing lipoprotein particles has reached a sufficiently high level, VLDL become IDL and then LDL. The IDL therefore could be considered as intermediate products between the VLDL and the LDL[1]. The main physiological function of the LDL is to carry cholesterol and deliver it to the body cells where it is needed; a more detailed description of this function is given below.

High Density Lipoproteins (HDL)

The biogenesis of the HDL remains obscure (Fig 40). They seem to originate in the liver where, as nascent particles, they have the form of discs and are rich in Apo E[4]. They then enter into the blood circulation where they acquire their main components (Figs 39 and 40). Some of these components are synthesized in the liver while others originate in the intestine. Here again, lecithin-cholesterol-acyl-transferase (LCAT) may be responsible for the synthesis of cholesterol esters present in HDL. Apo A forms the major part of the apolipoproteins characteristic of HDL; these apolipoproteins come from the liver and from exchanges with other lipoproteins circulating in the blood[2,3,5-7]. Latest information[8-10], however, would give the intestine a major role in the formation of Apo A-I, the major apolipoprotein of HDL. Apo A-I appears in chylomicrons and is concentrated at the surface of the remnants (Fig 39).

The formation of HDL is complex, as is obvious from the above, and is based on metabolic processes of a different nature. Other investigations will therefore be necessary to clarify completely the origin and the processes by which HDL are formed in the body. The physiological functions of these lipoproteins which will be discussed later in this chapter are still not well understood.

THE FUNCTIONS OF LIPOPROTEINS

As mentioned earlier, lipoproteins are involved in the transport of lipids in the blood. Chylomicrons and VLDL are the main carriers of triglycerides, and LDL and HDL are the main carriers of cholesterol. The carrying of triglycerides to the body tissues by chylomicrons and VLDL has been described and was illustrated in Figs 39 and 40. Only the transport of cholesterol, therefore, the main function of LDL and HDL, will be reviewed here.

To multiply, grow and maintain their integrity, all body cells need a steady supply of cholesterol. It is also essential for the formation and proper functioning of all cellular and sub-cellular membranes[1] and is the precursor of several compounds essential to life. The proper functioning of each body cell therefore depends upon a vital equilibrium which must be maintained between the input and the output of cholesterol both at the cellular and whole body levels. The body cells, however, need to be protected against an excessive accumulation of cholesterol which might become damaging.

Most recent data indicate that the main function of LDL is to transport cholesterol to all cells throughout the body, including those of the arterial walls, and thus to ensure a steady input of cholesterol. Fig 41 shows some of the phenomena associated with this function[1,3,4,11]. Cholesterol may come from the diet or it may be synthesized in the liver, but when it is incorporated into LDL it is mainly in the form of cholesterol ester (CE). LDL also contain some free cholesterol (FC), phospholipids and proteins, mainly, Apo B.

It has been clearly shown[11] that the cell membrane has specific receptors for LDL-Apo B. Through Apo B, LDL adhere to the cell membrane and then are absorbed probably by pinocytosis (Fig 41). Up to 10,000 receptors can usually be counted on the membrane of one cell.

Once they are absorbed by the cell, the LDL particles meet the lysosomes which are the carriers of specific enzymes causing the hydrolysis of Apo B. The hydrolysis causes the disintegration of the LDL globules and the release of the cholesterol esters. Other specific enzymes catalyze the hydrolysis of these cholesterol esters to yield free cholesterol and fatty acids. The free cholesterol then becomes available for its various essential cellular functions.

However, a too abundant accretion of free cholesterol would constitute a danger to the survival of the body cells. That is perhaps why nature gave

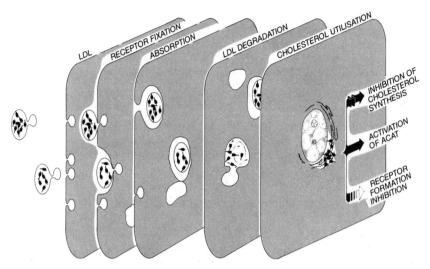

Fig. 41—Diagram showing the function of LDL as the carriers of cholesterol to the body cells.

(Based on references[1,3,4,11].)

The main function of LDL is to transport cholesterol from the liver to the body cells. Cell membranes have specific receptors for LDL Apo B. The attached LDL then penetrate into the cells where they are disintegrated to deliver their content of cholesterol esters. The cholesterol esters are hydrolyzed and free cholesterol becomes available for the formation or the maintenance of sub-cellular membranes and to serve as the precursor of needed molecules.

free cholesterol three remarkable properties. As it accumulates in the cells, free cholesterol:

* slows down the biosynthesis of new cholesterol molecules within the cells by inhibiting the enzyme HMG-CoA reductase (hydroxy-methyl-glutaryl CoA reductase), an enzyme involved in the synthesis of an intermediate precursor of cholesterol;
* slows down the synthesis of the Apo B receptors on the cell membrane; consequently the absorption of additional LDL is inhibited;
* stimulates the re-esterification of cholesterol; the amount of free cholesterol is then proportionately reduced. This reaction is under the control of an enzyme named acyl CoA: cholesterol acyltransferase (ACAT) which is specific for the saturated and monounsaturated fatty acids.

According to most recent data, the main function of LDL in man could therefore be described as follows: LDL ensure the transport of cholesterol from the liver to the body cells where it is essential for both the proper functioning of each cell and the survival of the whole organism.

The mechanism by which the esterified cholesterol is returned to the liver is still not clear. Hypotheses have been put forth which might have important consequences if they are confirmed. According to these hypotheses, the HDL would be the carriers of cholesterol from the body cells to the liver from where it could be eliminated. Because of such hypotheses, HDL have attracted much attention as they could possibly protect against atherosclerosis and cardiovascular disease.

There are two pools of cholesterol in the human body. The first consists of the cholesterol found in erythrocytes, liver, spleen and ileum; the second is the cholesterol entering all other tissues and organs including adipose tissue, arterial walls and muscles. In the human body, the size of these two pools is not influenced by the concentration of cholesterol, triglycerides, VLDL or LDL in the blood. However, the amounts of cholesterol found in these two pools would be inversely related to the concentration of HDL-cholesterol[12]: the higher the concentration of HDL-cholesterol in blood, the lower the concentration of cholesterol in these two pools.

This inverse relationship became the basis of a hypothesis put forward to explain the role of HDL in the body: to carry cholesterol from the body cells and tissues to the liver where it is excreted. This would be consistent with the apparent protective effects of HDL-cholesterol against atherosclerosis and ischemic heart disease. But this is simply a hypothesis which has yet to be confirmed.

If this hypothesis is confirmed, it could then be stated that HDL are the carriers of cholesterol from the body tissues to the liver where it is transformed into bile acids and then excreted via the bile into the intestine, the main route through which it leaves the body. Thus, HDL would play an extremely important role in regulating the amount of cholesterol retained in all body tissues, including arterial walls. Such a function would give HDL important antiatherogenic properties and establish its role in the prevention of ischemic heart disease. Among other things this could explain why, as will be seen later, persons with a high HDL blood level seem to be less prone to cardiovascular disease.

Other functions of the circulating lipoproteins are associated with the nature of their apolipoproteins. For example, the Apo C of VLDL and HDL activates lipoprotein lipase (LPL) and the Apo A of HDL activates lecithin-cholesterol-acyl-transferase (LCAT)[6]. These particular functions have already been mentioned.

LIPOPROTEINS AND CORONARY HEART DISEASE

The concentration of total cholesterol in the blood serum, as was seen in Chapter 4, is statistically correlated with the risk of coronary heart disease. However, it is known, although not universally accepted, that using blood cholesterol levels to gauge the likelihood of a given subject developing atherosclerosis cannot be relied upon in the detection of cardiovascular disease[12-18]. Mann[13] and Carlson[17] have seriously questioned the value of the serum cholesterol level as an indicator of cardiovascular disease for a given subject. One might be inclined to agree with them when examining closely Fig 42. This figure was based on the data of the Framingham Study[18]. It shows the distribution curves for the blood cholesterol

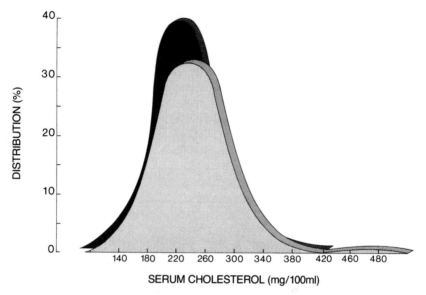

Fig. 42—Distribution curves of the blood cholesterol levels in two groups of men, with and without coronary heart disease.

(Adapted from Kannel, Castelli and Gordon[18].)

This figure shows the distribution curves of blood cholesterol levels in 1,571 men aged 30–49 years included in the Framingham Study. One curve applies to the men declared healthy and the other to those suffering from coronary heart disease. The healthy subjects had an average serum cholesterol level of 219 ± 41.4 mg per 100 ml as compared to 244 ± 51.4 mg for those suffering from coronary heart disease. The difference between these two values is not statistically significant. Therefore statistically these two groups of men belong to the same population. In fact, it can be seen that the two curves overlap and practically cover the same area. As a result, we are led to conclude that the total blood cholesterol level is not a reliable index for measuring the risk that a given subject will suffer from coronary heart disease.

levels in two different groups of men aged 39–49 years. One group includes men declared healthy and the other includes men known to have coronary heart disease. The distribution of the blood cholesterol levels is practically identical in both groups; the two curves overlap and practically cover the same area.

These facts suggest the following conclusions.

> *Total cholesterol in the blood cannot be used as a reliable index to distinguish between healthy men and men suffering from coronary heart disease. Many physicians and investigators have already expressed this view*[12–20].

Cholesterol in blood is almost entirely incorporated into the various categories of lipoproteins: VLDL, LDL and HDL. The LDL alone carry 65–70 per cent of total blood cholesterol and the HDL, 20–25 per cent. Thus, the various types of lipoproteins as possible risk factors for coronary heart disease have been the object of many investigations during the past decade. We will review the most pertinent data on the subject and discuss nutritional and other factors that may influence the concentration of the respective lipoproteins in blood.

Blood VLDL and triglycerides

VLDL and chylomicrons are the major carriers of triglycerides in the blood (see earlier). When chylomicrons are cleared, after a few hours of fasting, the VLDL become the principal carriers of endogenous triglycerides. Many investigations have evaluated the fasting blood triglyceride levels as possible risk factors for cardiovascular disease. Many of the investigations showed a significant correlation between the concentration of triglycerides in blood and the risk of coronary heart disease[16,18,20–28]. These studies, however, did not take into account other risk factors that might explain this correlation. In a recent study[29], the association between blood triglycerides and coronary heart disease has been examined using statistical methods that take into account other risk factors such as blood cholesterol, HDL, body mass, cigarette smoking and systolic blood pressure.

This latter study was based on data derived from the Western Collaborative Group Study and demonstrated that the association between blood triglycerides and coronary heart disease can be explained by other risk factors.

The conclusion reached by the authors of this study[29] deserves to be quoted:

> *"We judge that the widespread practice of identifying and treating hypertriglyceridemia in apparently healthy persons for the*

purpose of preventing coronary heart disease is inappropriate
unless more persuasive evidence becomes available".[29]

Therefore, intervention programs based on modifications to the diet,
aimed at lowering the blood triglyceride levels so as to reduce the risk of
cardiovascular disease, are not justified. The data from the Coronary Drug
Project also confirm this view[30].

As the VLDL are the main carriers of endogenous triglycerides,
it is clear that this class of lipoproteins could not be considered
as a risk factor for coronary heart disease on the basis of their
triglyceride content.

Since the VLDL are no more reliable than triglycerides as indicators
of the risk for coronary heart disease, a discussion of the dietary factors
which might influence their concentration in blood is of little interest here.

LDL and total blood cholesterol

The LDL are the carriers of more than two thirds of the blood cholesterol. About 2,000 mg of cholesterol is incorporated into these lipoproteins and delivered to body cells each day[4]. Since they carry 65–70 per
cent of the total cholesterol in the blood, any factor that affects the LDL
levels in blood tends to affect also total cholesterol levels. Similarly, data
obtained in studies dealing with total blood cholesterol are also relevant
to LDL-cholesterol. It has been clearly demonstrated that LDL-cholesterol
is always high when total blood cholesterol is high and always low when
total blood cholesterol is low[18,31]. Fig 43 shows the close relationship
between total blood cholesterol and LDL-cholesterol.

One of the implications of such a relationship is that the scientific data
which have been accumulated on the relationship between total blood
cholesterol and coronary heart disease also apply to LDL-cholesterol[20].
Similarly, any treatment or change in the diet which would lower blood
cholesterol would also lower LDL-cholesterol. For these reasons it would
appear unnecessary to distinguish between total blood cholesterol and
LDL-cholesterol when studying the risks for coronary heart disease. The
same could be said for any prevention intervention program. Therefore in
this book, remarks and conclusions regarding total blood cholesterol also
apply to LDL-cholesterol and vice versa. When in 1979 Carlson wrote:
"Let total serum-cholesterol be retired after its long service"[17] he might
have said the same about LDL-cholesterol.

HDL-cholesterol or the "good" cholesterol

As mentioned above, HDL are believed to be the carriers of cholesterol
from the body cells, including those in the arterial walls, to the liver. In

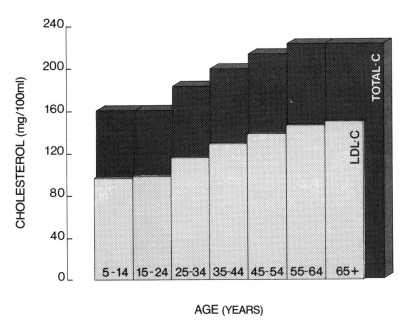

Fig. 43—Association between LDL-cholesterol and total blood cholesterol.

(Adapted from Rifkind et al.[31].)

There is a close association between the concentrations of LDL-cholesterol and total cholesterol in the blood; this association can be observed in both sexes. As 65–70 per cent of blood cholesterol is transported in the form of LDL, any factor affecting the LDL blood levels will influence total cholesterol in a similar manner. In the same way, data obtained in studies dealing with total blood cholesterol would also apply to LDL-cholesterol. Any conclusion concerning the influence of diet or other factors on LDL-cholesterol also applies to total blood cholesterol and vice versa.

the liver, cholesterol is transformed into bile acids and is excreted into the intestine. This new role of HDL, as suggested by Miller and Miller[12], could explain practically all the scientific observations made since 1975 relating the risk for coronary heart disease to the lipoprotein levels in blood[16,32,33].

This role, for example, could explain the inverse relationship observed between the concentration of the circulating HDL and the incidence of cardiovascular disease[16,19,34]. To illustrate the negative correlation between HDL and coronary heart disease, data from the Framingham study were used (Fig 44). In this study, the concentration of HDL-cholesterol in blood was plotted against the incidence of coronary heart disease[34]. Note that the incidence is nearly 140 cases per 1,000 when the HDL-cholesterol is 30 mg per 100 ml but is only 20 cases per 1,000 when HDL-cholesterol rises to 70 mg per 100 ml.

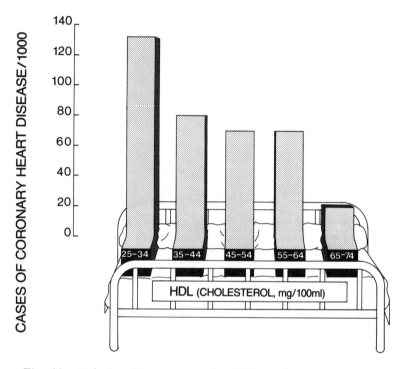

Fig. 44—Relationship between the HDL-cholesterol levels in blood and the incidence of coronary heart disease (HDL expressed as mg of cholesterol per 100 ml).

(Adapted from Gordon *et al*[34].)

This diagram illustrates the inverse relationship that exists between the HDL-cholesterol levels in blood and the incidence of coronary heart disease and is based on the data reported from the Framingham Study. The incidence of coronary heart disease gradually decreased as the HDL-cholesterol level in blood increased. The incidence was nearly 140 cases per 1,000 at the level of 30 mg HDL-cholesterol per 100 ml of serum, and dropped to only 20 cases when the level was 70 mg per 100 ml. Such observations served as a basis for the belief that HDL is a protective factor against coronary heart disease.

Similar observations were made in several other studies in the past few years[12,14,16,32,33,35]. Many researchers now believe that HDL may be a protective factor against coronary heart disease, probably by slowing the progress of atherosclerosis. It is not surprising, then, to see a rapidly growing interest in this class of lipoproteins.

The relationship that exists between the HDL-cholesterol levels and the incidence of coronary heart disease was precisely defined in a study involving five different populations, totalling 6,859 subjects[16]. This major investigation is referred to as the Cooperative Lipoprotein Phenotyping Study. It was shown once more that the incidence of coronary heart disease diminished as the HDL-cholesterol levels in blood increased. Serum HDL-cholesterol in healthy subjects was 3–4 mg per 100 ml higher than in subjects with clinical signs of coronary heart disease, a difference of approximately 10 per cent. Such a difference is rather small but it was observed repeatedly in each study dealing with this subject and it is statistically significant.

However, a statistically significant difference between two variables does not automatically mean a cause-and-effect relationship between them. Furthermore, the fact that a difference between two variables is statistically significant gives no indication as to its importance in practice, that is in our everyday life.

An examination of the normal distribution curve of serum HDL in a given population may give some clues as to the practical importance of an increase in HDL of about 10 per cent in serum. Fig 45 shows the normal distribution curve of HDL concentration in the blood of a population of 2,568 men aged 25–65. The HDL-cholesterol levels in the serum range from 35 to more than 90 mg per 100 ml. The average for this group of men is 55 mg with a standard deviation of ± 12 mg.

It may be worthwhile to note that the normal distribution curve of blood HDL shown in Fig 45 is similar from many points of view to the normal distribution curve for total blood cholesterol (Fig 29). This means that the HDL concentration in the blood of many individuals with coronary heart disease will fall within the range of that of healthy individuals. Under these conditions, one can expect to see an important overlap of the HDL concentrations in healthy subjects over those found in subjects suffering from coronary heart disease. Effectively, such an overlap has been observed in Norway[32]. In spite of these variations and overlaps, many researchers, physicians and other health professionals would agree with the following conclusion:

An increase in HDL is associated with a reduction of the risk of atherosclerosis and coronary heart disease; HDL blood levels therefore may be a useful criterion for evaluating the risk for this kind of degenerative disease.

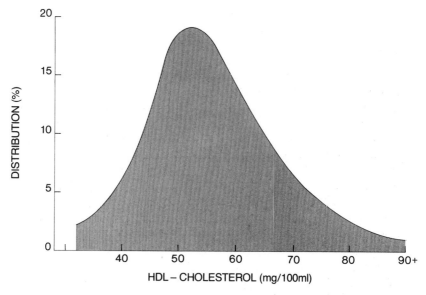

*Fig. 45—Normal distribution curve of the HDL-cholesterol levels
in the blood of a group of men aged 25–65.*

(Taken from Williams, Robinson and Bailey[35].)

This normal distribution curve shows that the concentration of
HDL in the blood serum of 25–65 year-old men ranges from less
than 35 mg to more than 90 mg per 100 ml. The average is 55 mg
with a standard deviation of ± 12 mg. In practical terms, such a
distribution curve indicates that wide variations are expected from
one man to another within this population. An important overlap
is also expected of the HDL concentrations in the blood of healthy
subjects over those found in subjects suffering from coronary heart
disease. In spite of these variations and overlaps, many investigators, physicians and other health professionals believe that HDL
protect against atherosclerosis and coronary heart disease.

FACTORS INFLUENCING THE HDL LEVELS IN BLOOD

Many investigators have already noted that severe atherosclerosis and
cardiovascular disease are often found in subjects with serum cholesterol
levels considered normal[12,18]. It has also been observed that in these patients, the HDL-cholesterol levels always tend to be lower than in healthy
individuals. In the light of these observations, the Miller and Miller hypothesis[12] to the effect that the HDL are protective factors against ischemic
heart disease has influenced many investigations carried out with the object

of identifying the factors affecting the HDL-cholesterol levels in blood. The following factors have been studied and will be discussed: sex, physical exercise, cigarette smoking, obesity, alcohol consumption and diet.

Sex and serum HDL

The HDL blood levels in women are always higher than in men. This was noted in the Framingham Study[34]. For subjects older than 50, the HDL level in women is 17–31 per cent higher than in men (Table 15). A difference of nearly 35 per cent between sexes, in subjects aged 30–70 years, has also been reported by Swedish investigators. In men, the serum HDL levels remain constant between 50 and 80 years of age whereas in women, the levels drop gradually[34,36–38]. It is more and more evident that the HDL levels in men are lower than in women[34,36–41]. This difference in HDL levels could explain, in part, why men are more at risk to atherosclerosis and ischemic heart disease than women.

Obesity and serum HDL

Body mass, as an index of obesity, has a significant influence on the HDL level in blood. This influence has been demonstrated in an experiment carried out in Italy[42] and summarized in Fig 46. When body weight is expressed in Index Body Weight units and HDL as Apo A-I, blood HDL decreases as body weight increases. This inverse relationship between serum HDL and body weight can be observed both in men and in women.

TABLE 15

SERUM HDL LEVELS AS A FUNCTION OF AGE
IN MEN AND WOMEN (expressed as mg
of cholesterol per 100 ml)*

Age	Men	Women	Difference (%)
50–59	45	59	31
60–69	46	57	24
70–79	47	55	17

* Data taken from Gordon et al[34]

Women in general have higher serum HDL levels than men, the levels tending to decrease with age, while in men they remain constant. Lower serum HDL levels in men than in women could explain why man is more prone than woman to atherosclerosis and ischemic heart disease

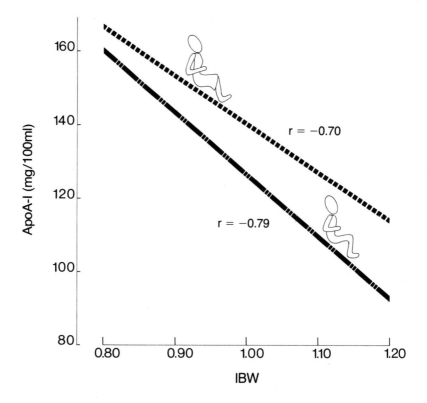

Fig. 46—Relationship between body weight and blood HDL
(body weight expressed as Index Body Weight units and HDL
as mg of Apo A-I per 100 ml of serum).

(From Avogaro et al[42].)

An inverse relationship between body weight related to ideal weight (IBW) and serum HDL has been reported in many if not all publications dealing with this subject. In general, the HDL levels tend to decrease as body weight increases. In this figure, the inverse relationship between IBW and HDL is statistically highly significant. Unfortunately, this relationship has not always been as marked in other studies. Furthermore, in many cases, the HDL levels in subjects maintained on a reducing diet tend to drop momentarily and to return to their initial values after a certain period. More investigations are needed to define more precisely the influence of overweight on blood HDL.

The correlation coefficients, −0.79 for men and −0.70 for women, are statistically highly significant.

If the inverse relationship between HDL and body weight observed in the above experiment were extrapolated to the public at large, a high HDL level could be expected in individuals maintaining ideal body weight. Unfortunately, other studies have shown that the inverse relationship between obesity and serum HDL, although statistically significant, remains feeble and not too important from the practical point of view. That is the reason why in many cases increased body weight or obesity has been observed to have only a minute lowering influence on the HDL blood levels. Nevertheless, the inverse relationship between body weight, obesity or body mass and blood HDL has been observed in almost all studies dealing with this subject[33,38,39,42−48].

From the practical point of view, it has been shown that weight loss associated with a reduction in the calorie intake could be temporarily accompanied by an undesirable lowering of HDL[44]; this is followed by a gradual increase to the initial levels after several months even though weight loss may persist (Table 16). It appears therefore that lowering body weight in obese subjects by submitting them to a low calorie diet does not ensure a rise in blood HDL, although the inverse relationship between HDL and body weight index has been noted in many investigations.

In the light of these observations, it is clear that additional research, carried out under more diversified and better controlled conditions, is needed before the practical implications of the association between obesity and the HDL blood levels are understood. Nevertheless it can be stated that in the population at large the blood HDL levels tend to increase as

TABLE 16

BODY WEIGHT CHANGES AND SERUM HDL IN WOMEN
AGED 25–55, MAINTAINED ON A REDUCING DIET*.

Time of weighing	Body weight (kg)	Serum HDL-cholesterol (mg per 100 ml)
Start	105	50
After 10 weeks	95	45
After 8 months	92	53

* Data taken from Thompson et al[44]

A reducing diet may temporarily lower rather than increase blood HDL levels. After several months of dieting, however, the HDL levels gradually return to the initial values. This observation reduces the likelihood of being able to increase blood HDL in obese persons by means of low-calorie diets.

the body weight index decreases. However, to what extent seeking to reduce the body weight index in the general public would help to reduce the tendency to atherosclerosis and the incidence of coronary heart disease through increased levels of blood HDL, is far from known.

Exercise and serum HDL

People exercising regularly have higher blood HDL levels than sedentary people. The difference in serum HDL between highly active and sedentary subjects varies between 15 and 50 per cent. These differences were observed for the first time in skiers, runners and lumberjacks[49-51]. These initial reports concerning the effect of exercise on blood HDL were encouraging and certainly helped to promote jogging. Unfortunately the data so far accumulated were not always unexceptionable. For example, it is possible that people following vigorous jogging and/or body fitness programs are also people who give thought to their diet and their health in general. Furthermore, the data accumulated to date concerning the effect of exercise on blood HDL seldom if ever make it possible to distinguish between the effects of exercise proper and the effects of cigarette smoking, obesity, alcohol drinking, daily relaxation and so forth[52,53]. Many of the observations published up to now could have arisen from many variables other than physical activity.

In a recent report[54], however, a relationship was noted between the maximum aerobic capacity in men and serum HDL-cholesterol. This observation could be interpreted as indirect evidence for the influence that a body fitness program might have on blood HDL. Nevertheless, additional research with appropriate study designs will have to be planned and carried out before a clear distinction can be made between the effects of physical activity and those of other factors on blood HDL. Similarly, from a practical point of view, more data are needed before a dependable evaluation can be made regarding the influence of physical activity on the development of atherosclerosis and the incidence of coronary heart disease.

Cigarette smoking and serum HDL

Cigarette smoking increases the risk of coronary heart disease, as was demonstrated in many studies carried out in different countries[43,55-61]. One reason why cigarette smoking is a risk factor for coronary heart disease might be that smoking is accompanied by a lowering of serum HDL[35,43,62]. Fig 47 shows, for example, that cigarette smokers have lower serum HDL levels than non-smokers. In men, the difference between smokers and non-smokers is 4 mg per 100 ml; in women, it is 6 mg. Furthermore, the reduction of serum HDL associated with smoking seems to be proportional to the number of cigarettes smoked daily. The HDL-lowering effect of

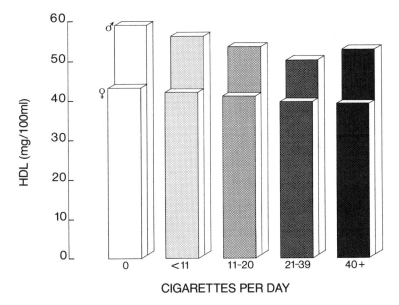

Fig. 47—Effect of cigarette smoking on serum HDL (expressed as mg of cholesterol per 100 ml).

(Adapted from Garrison *et al*[43].)

Cigarette smoking lowers the concentration of HDL in blood. This effect is proportional to the number of cigarettes smoked daily. The difference between the serum HDL levels in smokers and non-smokers is greater in men than in women but it does not exceed a maximum value of about 15 per cent. Cigarette smoking therefore seems to have a real effect on serum HDL. For this reason cigarette smoking is one of the risk factors for coronary heart disease.

---

smoking, however, is not greater than about 15 per cent when a comparison is made with non-smokers.

In most investigations carried out on the effect of smoking, a distinction was made between the effect of smoking *per se* and that of other factors such as physical activity, obesity, alcohol and so on. The effect of smoking therefore could be singled out and was not confounded with that of other factors.

Under these conditions, it can be concluded that smoking has a real effect on serum HDL and that it is really a risk factor for coronary heart disease. It is still too soon, however, to assess quantitatively the effect of the smoking habit on the coronary heart disease mortality.

Alcohol and serum HDL

Moderate alcohol consumption has been found to be associated with a lower risk of coronary heart disease. Moderate alcohol drinking was also associated with an increase in serum HDL. The data from a study carried out in the United States of America, the Cooperative Lipoprotein Phenotyping Study[63], can be used to illustrate these findings (Fig 48). The study involved 3,300 subjects aged 50–69. It was observed that serum HDL-cholesterol increased gradually as the consumption of alcohol increased.

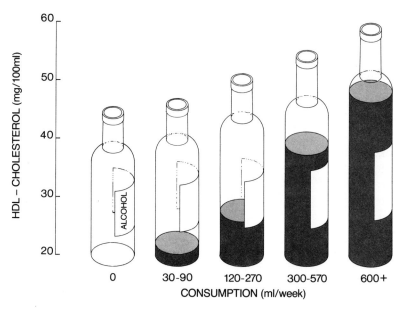

Fig. 48—Effect of alcohol drinking on serum HDL.

(Adapted from Castelli *et al*[63].)

The concentration of HDL in serum increases in proportion to the daily consumption of alcohol taken in the form of beer, wine or spirits. The difference between the levels of serum HDL in tee-totallers and in those consuming 600 ml or more of alcohol per week is 35 per cent. The effect of alcohol drinking on serum HDL can be observed in women as well as in men. Furthermore, it appears to be proportional to the amount consumed. Based on the data presented in this figure, one might predict that, in a given population, an average consumption of 300 ml of alcohol per week might bring about an increase in serum HDL of about 25 per cent when compared to a population of teetotallers. A moderate consumption of alcohol therefore is a factor contributing to increased HDL levels in blood.

The difference between the levels of serum HDL in teetotallers and in those drinking 600 ml of alcohol or more per week was nearly 35 per cent; such a difference is considerable when compared to the effect of most other factors with an influence on serum HDL. The effect of drinking alcohol on the elevation of serum HDL can be observed in women as well as in men[38,43,63] and it is of about the same magnitude in both.

In addition, it appears that the effect of alcohol consumption on the HDL levels in serum is, to a certain extent, proportional to the amount consumed. On several occasions, in this book, we have been dealing with effects and associations which were sometimes statistically significant, sometimes non-significant and sometimes non-existent; we have often used expressions such as "it might be", "may be", "in certain cases", and "it would seem". We used such expressions, for example in the case of the effect of dietary cholesterol and polyunsaturated fatty acids (PUFA) on blood cholesterol. In the case of alcohol consumption, however, the effect on serum HDL is truly proportional to the amount consumed within the range of consumption appearing in Fig 48. One could therefore predict the increase in serum HDL, knowing the quantity of alcohol consumed per week. For example, one might predict that the consumption of 300 ml of alcohol per week in the form of beer, wine or spirits would bring about an increase in serum HDL of about 25 per cent in a population of drinkers when compared to a population of non-drinkers.

From a practical point of view, it would be of interest to examine the effect of moderate alcohol consumption on coronary heart disease mortality. An example may be found in an investigation carried out in Hawaii on 7,700 men[64]. In these subjects, none of whom consumed less than 300 ml of alcohol per week, the mortality due to coronary heart disease was 55 per cent lower than in teetotalers (Fig 49).

Of all the factors considered in this book, a moderate consumption of alcohol appears to have the greatest beneficial effect on coronary heart disease mortality. Present knowledge does not provide an explanation for this effect of alcohol consumption. Could it be simply the relaxation induced[65]? Even though the explanation is lacking, it will be difficult from now on to ignore this protective factor against coronary heart disease mortality in studies dealing with this most important cause of death.

On the other hand, nutrionists will have to exercise extreme caution if they recommend alcohol drinking as a protection against coronary heart disease, because there are too many disadvantages associated with this habit both from the health and the social point of view.

Diet and serum HDL

For the nutritionists, the effect of diet on the serum HDL levels remains a matter of major interest. Unfortunately the available data are too

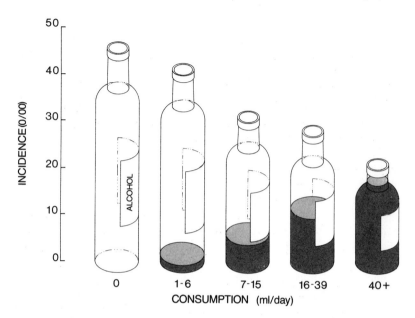

Fig. 49—*Effect of moderate consumption of alcohol on the incidence of coronary heart disease mortality.*

(Adapted from Yano, Rhoads and Kagan[64].)

Moderate consumption of alcohol is associated with a drop in the incidence of coronary heart disease mortality. The consumption of 300 ml of alcohol per week (40 ml per day) as compared to none is followed by a drop in mortality of 55 per cent. Of all factors considered in this book, the moderate consumption of alcohol appears to have the greatest influence on coronary heart disease mortality. Alcoholism, however, has serious effects both on health and on social life, so that it does not follow that the consumption of alcohol should be recommended to reduce the risk of coronary heart disease: but one fact remains, a moderate consumption of alcohol could be beneficial.

few yet to be able to answer all the questions on this subject. The first publications on the Multiple Risk Factor Intervention Trial (MRFIT), however, could be used as indications of the possible relationship between diet and serum HDL.

In this study, the diet of the participants was meant to provide less than 300 mg of cholesterol daily and less than 30–35 per cent of calories in the form of fat. Furthermore, the dietary fats were to contribute less than 10 per cent of total calories as saturated fatty acids and more than 10 per cent as polyunsaturated fatty acids[66]. After two years of intervention, the serum HDL levels in the participants had remained unchanged. The authors of the report concluded: "Neither the fat controlled diet nor the multifactor intervention program altered mean levels of this lipoprotein."[66] An identical conclusion was reached in another publication dealing with the same multiple intervention program[45].

The influence of polyunsaturated fatty acids (PUFA) on the concentration of serum HDL was investigated in eight subjects aged 19 to 23 years[67]. A diet based on safflower seed oil, to obtain a P/S ratio of 4.0, raised serum HDL by 20 per cent. Unfortunately, a diet having a P/S ratio of 4.0 is high in PUFA and may have unknown side-effects on health, as will be seen in chapter 7.

An experiment carried out in the Netherlands[68] led to the opposite conclusions. A diet rich in saturated fats significantly increased serum HDL whereas a diet high in polyunsaturated fat had no influence on this parameter. Another investigation carried out in Norway[69] indicated that a diet high in polyunsaturated fats as compared to a diet rich in saturated fats might increase slightly the serum HDL levels in hyperlipemic subjects. This study, however, can be easily criticized because the effect of the diet was confounded with behavioral changes occurring in the experimental subjects.

The effect of diet on serum HDL was studied in 116 vegetarians, 73 men and 43 women[70]. The vegetarian diet caused a drop in serum cholesterol as might be expected, but at the same time, it caused a drop in serum HDL. In these vegetarians, serum cholesterol was about 45 per cent lower than in nonvegetarians, but the HDL levels were also lower by 27 per cent. The effects of such changes in blood lipids on the incidence of coronary heart disease are still unknown, but it could well be that the simultaneous lowering of HDL might void the beneficial effects expected from the lowering of blood cholesterol. It is clear, however, that a vegetarian diet is not a means of elevating serum HDL.

In summary, the present knowledge concerning the effect of the diet on the levels of HDL in blood is insufficient to permit definite conclusions to be drawn in this regard. It appears, however, that changes in the nature of fats consumed by the general population could not be expected to increase the levels of HDL in blood.

REFERENCES

1. Goldstein JL, Brown MS: The low-density lipoprotein pathway and its relationship to atherosclerosis. *Ann Rev Biochem*, 46:897–930, 1977
2. Jackson RL, Morrisett JD, Gotto AM Jr: Lipoprotein structure and metabolism. *Physiol Rev*, 56:259–316, 1976

3. Grundy SM: Dietary fats and sterols. In Levy RI, Rifkind BM, Dennis BH, Ernst ND (eds) *Nutrition, Lipids, and Coronary Heart Disease. A Global View*. pp 89–118. New York, Raven Press, 1979
4. Steinberg D: Research related to under-

lying mechanisms in atherosclerosis. *Circulation*, 60:1559–1565, 1979

5. Pownall, HJ, Morrisett JD, Sparrow JT, Smith LC, Shepherd J, Jackson RL, Gotto AM Jr: A review of the unique feature of HDL apoproteins. *Lipids*, 14:428–434, 1979

6. Smith LC, Pownall HJ, Gotto AM Jr: The plasma lipoproteins: structure and metabolism. *Ann Rev Biochem*, 47:751–777, 1978

7. Morrisett JD, Jackson RL, Gotto AM Jr: Lipoproteins: structure and function. *Ann Rev Biochem*, 44:183–207, 1975

8. Tall AR, Green PHR, Glickman RM: Formation of high density lipoproteins from chylomicrons. *Circulation*, 57, 58(suppl. II):11–15, 1978

9. Redgrave TG, Small DM: Transfer of surface components of chylomicrons to the high density lipoprotein fraction during chylomicron catabolism in the rat. *Circulation*, 57, 58(suppl. II):11–14, 1978

10. Glickman RM: Intestinal lipoprotein formation. *Nutr Metab*, 24(suppl 1):3–11, 1980

11. Brown MS, Goldstein JL: Familial hypercholesterolemia: A genetic defect in the low-density lipoprotein receptor. *N Engl J Med*, 294:1386–1390, 1976

12. Miller GJ, Miller NE: Plasma-high-density-lipoprotein concentration and development of ischaemic heart-disease. *Lancet*, 1:16–19, 1975

13. Mann GV: Current concepts. Diet-heart: end of an era. *N Engl J Med*, 297:644–650, 1977

14. Miller NE, Thelle DS, Førde OH, Mjøs OD: The Tromsø heart-study. High-density lipoprotein and coronary heart-disease: a prospective case-control study. *Lancet*, 1:965–970, 1977

15. Anonyme: Blood lipids and coronary heart disease. *Nutr Rev*, 36:239–241, 1978

16. Castelli WP, Doyle JT, Gordon T, Hames CG, Hjortland MC, Hulley SB, Kagan A, Zukel WJ: HDL cholesterol and other lipids in coronary heart disease. The cooperative lipoprotein pheno-typing study. *Circulation*, 55:767–772, 1977

17. Carlson LA, Olsson AG: Serum-lipoprotein-cholesterol distribution in healthy men with high serum-cholesterol concentrations: extrapolation to clofibrate trial. *Lancet*, 1:869–870, 1979

18. Kannel WB, Castelli WP, Gordon T: Cholesterol in the prediction of atherosclerotic disease. New perspectives based on the Framingham study. *Ann Intern Med*, 90:85–91, 1979

19. Avogaro P, Cazzolato G, Bittolo Bon G, Quinci GB: Are apolipoproteins better discriminators than lipids for atherosclerosis? *Lancet*, 1:901–903, 1979

20. Wieland H, Seidel D, Wiegand V, Kreuser H: Serum lipoproteins and coronary artery disease (CAD). Comparison of the lipoprotein profile with the results of coronary angiography. *Atherosclerosis*, 36:269–280, 1980

21. Kannel WB, Castelli WP, Gordon T, McNamara PM: Serum cholesterol, lipoproteins, and the risk of coronary heart disease: the Framingham study. *Ann Intern Med*, 74:1–12, 1971

22. Goldstein JL, Hazzard WR, Schrott HG, Bierman EL, Motulsky AG: Hyperlipidemia in coronary heart disease. I. Lipid levels in 500 survivors of myocardial infarctions. *J Clin Invest*, 52:1533–1543, 1973

23. Wilhelmsen L, Wedel H, Tibblin G: Multivariate analysis of risk factors for coronary heart disease. *Circulation*, 48:950–958, 1973

24. Tibblin G, Wilhelmsen L, Werkö L: Risk factors for myocardial infarction and death due to ischemic disease and other causes. *Am J Cardiol*, 35:514–522, 1975

25. Robertson TL, Kato H, Gordon T, Kagan A, Rhoads GG, Land CE, Worth RM, Belsky JL, Dock DS, Miyanishi M, Kawamoto S: Epidemiologic studies of coronary heart disease and stroke in Japanese men living in Japan, Hawaii and California. Coronary heart disease risk factors in Japan and Hawaii. *Am J Cardiol*, 39:244–249, 1977

26. Wilhelmsen L, Bengtsson C, Elmfeldt D, Vedin A, Wilhelmsson C, Tibblin G, Lindqvist O, Wedel H: Multiple risk prediction of myocardial infarction in women as compared with men. *Br Heart J,* 39:1179–1185, 1977

27. Rhoads GG, Blackwelder WC, Stemmermann GN, Hayashi T, Kagan A: Coronary risk factors and autopsy findings in Japanese-American men. *Lab Invest,* 38:304–311, 1978

28. Tzagournis M: Triglycerides in clinical medicine. A review. *Am J Clin Nutr,* 31:1437–1452, 1978

29. Hulley SB, Rosenman RH, Bawol RD, Brand RJ: Epidemiology as a guide to clinical decisions. The association between triglyceride and coronary heart disease. *N Engl J Med,* 302:1383–1389, 1980

30. Coronary Drug Project Research Group: Natural history of myocardial infarction in the coronary drug project: long-term prognostic importance of serum lipid levels. *Am J Cardiol,* 42:489–498, 1978

31. Rifkind BM, Tamir I, Heiss G, Wallace RB, Tyroler HA: Distribution of high density and other lipoproteins in selected LRC prevalence study populations: A brief survey. *Lipids,* 14:105–112, 1979

32. Berg K, Børresen A-L, Dahlen G: Serum-high-density-lipoprotein and atherosclerotic heart-disease. *Lancet,* 1:499–505, 1976

33. Rhoads, GG, Gulbrandsen CL, Kagan A: Serum lipoproteins and coronary heart disease in a population study of Hawaii Japanese men. *N Engl J Med,* 294:293–298, 1976

34. Gordon T, Castelli WP, Hjortland MC, Kannel WB, Dawber TR: High density lipoprotein as a protective factor against coronary heart disease. The Framingham study. *Am J Med,* 62:707–714, 1977

35. Williams P, Robinson D, Bailey A: High-density lipoprotein and coronary risk factors in normal men. *Lancet,* 1:72–75, 1979

36. Avogaro P, Cazzolato G, Bittolo Bon G, Quinci GG: High and low high-density lipoproteins: clinical implications. *Nutr Metab,* 24(suppl 1):34–44, 1980

37. Avogaro P, Cazzolato G, Bittolo Bon G, Quinci GB: Values of apo-A, and apo-B in humans according to ages and sex. *Clinica Chim Acta,* 95:311–315, 1979

38. Yano Y, Irie N, Homma Y, Tsushima M, Takeuchi I, Nakaya N, Goto Y: High density lipoprotein cholesterol levels in the Japanese. *Atherosclerosis,* 36:173–181, 1980

39. Carlson LA, Ericsson M: Quantitative and qualitative serum lipoprotein analysis. Part I. Studies in healthy men and women. *Atherosclerosis,* 21:417–433, 1975

40. Albers JJ, Wahl PW, Cabana VG, Hazzard WR, Hoover JJ: Quantitation of apolypoprotein A-I of human plasma high density lipoprotein. *Metabolism,* 25:633–644, 1976

41. Goto Y: Hyperlipidemia and atherosclerosis in Japan. *Atherosclerosis,* 36:341–349, 1980

42. Avogaro P, Cazzolato G, Bittolo Bon G, Quinci GB, Chinello M, HDL-cholesterol, apolipoproteins A₁ and B. Age and index body weight. *Atherosclerosis,* 31:85–91, 1978

43. Garrison RJ, Kannel WB, Feinleib M, Castelli WP, McNamara PM, Padgett SJ: Cigarette smoking and HDL cholesterol. The Framingham offspring study. *Atherosclerosis,* 30:17–25, 1978

44. Thompson PD, Jeffery RW, Wing RR, Wood PD: Unexpected decrease in plasma high density lipoprotein cholesterol with weight loss. *Am J Clin Nutr,* 32:2016–2021, 1979

45. Hulley S, Ashman P, Kuller L, Lasser N, Sherwin R: HDL-cholesterol levels in the Multiple Risk Factor Intervention Trial (MRFIT) by the MRFIT research group. *Lipids,* 14:119–125, 1979

46. Hulley SB, Cohen R, Widdowson G: Plasma high-density lipoprotein cholesterol level. Influence of risk factor intervention. *JAMA,* 238:2269–2271, 1977

47. Berenson GS, Srinivasan SR, Frerichs RR, Webber LS: Serum high density

lipoprotein and its relationship to cardiovascular disease risk factor variables in children—The Bogalusa heart study. *Lipids*, 14:91–98, 1979

48. Laskarzewski P, Morrison JA, Mellies MJ, Kelly K, Gartside PS, Khoury P, Glueck CJ: Relationships of measurements of body mass to plasma lipoproteins in schoolchildren and adults. *Am J Epidemiol*, 111:395–406, 1980

49. Wood PD, Haskell WL: The effect of exercise on plasma high density lipoproteins. *Lipids*, 14:417–427, 1979

50. Wood PD, Haskell W, Klein H, Lewis S, Stern MP, Farquhar JW: The distribution of plasma lipoproteins in middle-aged male runners. *Metabolism*, 25:1249–1257, 1976

51. Krauss RM, Lindgren FT, Wood PD, Haskell WL, Albers JJ, Cheung MC: Differential increases in plasma high density lipoprotein subfractions and apolipoproteins. *Circulation*, 56(suppl III):4, 1977

52. Wood PD, Haskell WL, Stern MP, Lewis S, Perry C: Plasma lipoprotein distributions in male and female runners. *Ann NY Acad Sci*, 301:748–763, 1977

53. Hickey N, Mulcahy R, Bourke GJ, Graham I, Wilson-Davis K: Study of coronary risk factors related to physical activity in 15, 171 men. *Br Med J*, 214:507–509, 1975

54. Miller NE, Rao S, Lewis B, Bjørsvik G, Myhre K, Mjøs OD: High-density lipoprotein and physical activity. *Lancet* 1:111, 1979

55. Rosenberg L, Shapiro S, Kaufman DW, Slone D, Miettinen OS, Stolley PD: Cigarette smoking in relation to the risk of myocardial infarction in young women. Modifying influence of age and predisposing factors. *Intern J Epidemiol*, 9:57–63, 1980

56. Friedman GD: Cigarette smoking and coronary heart disease: new evidence and old reactions. *Am Heart J*, 99:398–399, 1980

57. Pooling Project Research Group: Relationship of blood pressure, serum cholesterol, smoking habit, relative weight and ECG abnormalities to incidence of major coronary events. Final report of the Pooling Project. *J Chronic Dis*, 31:201–306, 1978

58. Miettinen OS, Neff R, Jick H: Cigarette smoking and nonfatal myocardial infarction: rate ratio in relation to age, sex, and predisposing conditions. *Am J Epidemiol*, 103:30–36, 1936

59. Doll R, Peto R: Mortality in relation to smoking: 20 years' observation on male British doctors. *Br Med J*, 2:1525–1536, 1976

60. Bain C, Hennekens CH, Rosner B, Speizer FE, Jessee MJ: Cigarette consumption and deaths from coronary heart disease. *Lancet*, 1:1087–1088, 1978

61. Anonyme: Surgeon general's report on smoking and health. Department of Health, Education and Welfare, Washington, DC, 1979

62. Godbourt U, Medalie JH: Characteristics of smokers, non-smokers and ex-smokers among 10,000 adult males in Israel. II. Physiologic, biochemical and genetic characteristics. *Am J Epidemiol*, 105:75–86, 1977

63. Castelli WP, Gordon T, Hjortland MC, Kagan A, Doyle JT, Hames CG, Hulley SB, Zukel WJ: Alcohol and blood lipids. The cooperative lipoprotein phenotyping study. *Lancet*, 2:153–155, 1977

64. Yano K, Rhoads GG, Kagan A: Coffee, alcohol and risk of coronary heart disease among Japanese men living in Hawaii. *N Engl J Med*, 297:405–409, 1977

65. Haynes SG, Feinleib M, Kannel WB: The relationship of psychosocial factors to coronary heart disease in the Framingham study. III. Eight-year incidence of coronary heart disease. *Am J Epidemiol*, 111:37–58, 1980

66. Multiple Risk Factor Intervention Research Group: The Multiple Risk Factor Intervention Trial (MRFIT). A national study of primary prevention of coronary heart disease. *JAMA*, 235:825–827, 1976

67. Morrisett JD, Pownall HJ, Jackson RL, Segura R, Gotto AM, Taunton OD: Effects of polyunsaturated and satu-

rated fat diets on the chemical composition and thermotropic properties of human plasma lipoproteins. In Kunau WH, Holman RT (eds) *Polyunsaturated Fatty Acids,* ch 8, pp 139–161. Champaign, Illinois, American Oil Chemist's Society, 1977

68. Brussaard JH, Dallinga-thie G, Groot PHE, Katan MB: Effects of amount and type of dietary fat on serum lipids, lipoproteins and apolipoproteins in man. A controlled 8-week trial. *Atherosclerosis,* 36:515–527, 1980

69. Hjermann I, Enger SC, Helgeland A, Holme Leren P, Trygg K: The effect of dietary changes on high density lipoprotein cholesterol. The Oslo study. *Am J Med,* 66:105–109, 1979

70. Sacks, FM, Castelli WP, Donner A, Kass EH: Plasma lipids and lipoproteins in vegetarians and controls. *N Engl J Med,* 292:1148–1151, 1975

7

The major intervention studies

INTRODUCTION

Cardiovascular disease is the main cause of mortality in countries with a high standard of living such as Canada, the United States of America, Great Britain and Scandinavia. Atherosclerosis appears to be the principal underlying condition responsible for the clinical manifestations of cardiovascular diseases and other circulatory disorders, heart attacks and sudden death. Atherosclerosis is characterized by the presence in the arterial walls of lipid-rich deposits. These deposits can cause partial or even complete occlusion of certain arteries. It is still impossible to prevent the formation of atherosclerotic deposits or to induce their regression. Despite 200 years of observation and research, the cause of atherosclerosis remains largely unknown and it is still impossible, for all practical purposes, to modify to any great degree its course or avoid its consequences[1].

Many epidemiological studies have identified a number of factors having at least a mathematical relationship to coronary heart disease. These are called risk factors for coronary heart disease[2-11]. Among these factors, the commonest are: high serum cholesterol, high blood pressure, cigarette smoking, heredity, obesity, and diabetes[1,12].

High serum cholesterol levels have frequently been observed in association with coronary heart disease[6,13,14]. Persons with a high serum cholesterol level have a higher risk of coronary heart disease than those with a low cholesterol level. Thus, the major intervention studies evaluated principally the effect of lowering serum cholesterol on the incidence of cardiovascular disease. In fact, the lipid hypothesis presupposes that a lowering of the blood cholesterol levels should be accompanied by a reduction of coronary heart disease mortality*.

---

* See Chapter 4.

143

Certain animal experiments suggested that blood cholesterol could be reduced by modifying the diet. Certain drugs such as clofibrate can also reduce blood cholesterol in man. Consequently the effects of diet and medication were the two main approaches evaluated in the major intervention studies.

In this chapter a review of the major intervention studies will be presented. A distinction will be made between primary and secondary preventions. Primary prevention interventions were designed for subjects who had not shown any clinical signs of coronary disorder at the beginning of the studies. The objective was to delay the onset or reduce the incidence of coronary heart disease. Secondary prevention interventions were designed for patients who had already shown signs of impaired cardiac circulation. Secondary prevention was thus aimed at retarding or even preventing relapses.

PRIMARY PREVENTION STUDIES

In the past fifteen years, four studies have been conducted in Chicago, New York, Los Angeles and Helsinki. The aim of the studies was to show that certain modifications of the diet could result in a lowering of serum cholesterol and, as a consequence, in a reduction of mortality from coronary heart disease. These four studies, stemming from the lipid hypothesis, were thus designed to determine the ability of diet to lower the blood cholesterol level, a possibility suggested some years earlier.

Another important primary prevention intervention was based on the hypocholesterolemic properties of clofibrate and was carried out in three European cities: Edinburgh, Budapest and Prague. This intervention was also inspired by the lipid hypothesis and its purpose was to evaluate whether the incidence of ischemic heart disease could be reduced in men aged 30–59 years if their serum cholesterol levels were lowered by means of medication; in this case clofibrate was used as a serum-cholesterol-lowering drug.

In the course of these extensive primary interventions, observations were made on 13,910 men aged 30–89 years at the beginning of the studies which lasted 4–8 years. An impressive mass of data was thus collected and the results should have led us to reliable conclusions.

Effect of changes in the lipid composition of the diet

Modifications of the diet evaluated in these studies included the reduction of cholesterol and saturated fatty acids intake on the one hand, and the increase of PUFA, polyunsaturated fatty acids, intake on the other*. The subjects requested to consume the high PUFA diet had an intake of cholesterol varying between 100 and 146 mg per 1,000 kcal per day, whereas control subjects had an intake of cholesterol higher by a factor of 170–200 per cent[15,16]. The P/S ratio of the fat portion of the diets varied from 1.25 to 1.78 for the high PUFA diets, as compared to a P/S ratio of from 0.2 to 0.3 for the control diets. Thus, polyunsaturated fatty acids contributed 10–15 per cent of total calories in the experimental diet as compared to 4–6 per cent in the control diets.

The changes in the diet in the majority of cases induced less than a 10 per cent lowering of serum cholesterol level (Table 17) which was significant from the biostatistical standpoint. The extent of this lowering effect on serum cholesterol was similar to that observed in other experiments mentioned in Chapter 5. It thus becomes evident that the decrease in serum cholesterol due to a drastic change in the fat composition of the diet cannot much exceed 10 per cent of the initial value.

It was also of interest to follow the changes in serum cholesterol during these interventions. In this respect, the Los Angeles Study[16] was particularly informative. This study lasted eight years, and the results obtained were similar in all respects to those reported from other major intervention studies.

It must be noted first of all that the greatest drop in serum cholesterol happened as soon as the subjects started on the low cholesterol high PUFA diet (Fig. 50). The effects of the changes in diet on blood cholesterol, as in other studies, were maximum during the first weeks of the intervention. In fact, it is always during the first weeks that the difference in serum cholesterol is greatest between the experimental subjects and the controls. Thereafter, serum cholesterol levels in both groups follow a similar pattern. Towards the end of the intervention, however, the differences between both groups taper off and, after eight years, are not statistically significant.

For the entire experimental period, the difference between blood cholesterol in both groups was 12 per cent, but this value fell to only 4 per cent after eight years of intervention. This observation would cast much doubt on the long-term effectiveness of changes in the fat composition of the diet in lowering blood cholesterol.

The reduction in blood cholesterol in the subjects consuming the high-PUFA low-cholesterol diet compared to controls was statistically significant in all intervention studies reported in Table 17. It thus becomes interesting to review the effect on mortality of lowering blood cholesterol. A critical examination of the way these interventions were conducted shows that for three out of five the verdict must be: "*Not conclusive*" (Table 17). The results on mortality are not conclusive because of some

---

* *A polyunsaturated fatty acid-rich diet is always high in linoleic acid (C18:2ω6) and low in fat of animal origin.*

TABLE 17

SUMMARY OF PRIMARY PREVENTION STUDIES BASED ON CHANGES IN THE FAT COMPOSITION OF THE DIET OR ON THE USE OF A SERUM CHOLESTEROL LOWERING DRUG

Source	Diet or drug	Dietary cholesterol[1]	P/S	Length (years)	No. of men (age)	Δ CHOL[2]	Effect on mortality
Chicago[17]	Low in SFA Low in CHOL Low in calories	?	?	5	519 (40–59)	−15	Not conclusive; deficient experimental design, no control group.
Los Angeles[16]	Low in SFA High in PUFA Low in CHOL	146	1.75 vs 0.24[3]	8	846 (30–59)	−13	No effect on mortality; more cancer with high PUFA diet.
New York Anti Coronary Club[18]	Low in SFA High in PUFA Low in CHOL	?	1.25–1.50	7	1,242 (40–59)	−8	Not conclusive; deficient experimental design.
Helsinki[15,19]	Low in SFA High in PUFA Low in CHOL	100	1.42–1.78 vs 0.22–0.29	6	676 (34–64)	−15	Total mortality identical in both groups.
Edinburgh Budapest Prague[20]	Clofibrate (1.6 g/d)	—	—	5	10,627 (30–59)	−9	No effect on mortality; more cancers and gallstones in treated subjects.

[1] Dietary cholesterol as mg/1,000 kcal per day
[2] Change in serum cholesterol level as per cent of controls
[3] Control diet

SFA : saturated fatty acids
PUFA : polyunsaturated fatty acids
CHOL : dietary cholesterol

Five extensive primary prevention intervention studies were carried out in the hope of showing that major changes in the fat composition of the diet or the use of a serum-cholesterol-lowering drug would reduce mortality from cardiovascular disease in the population at large. Neither the changes in the diet nor the drug had any influence on mortality. In some studies, apart from cardiovascular effects, there were more cancers in individuals eating the high PUFA diet than in controls; in other cases undesirable side-effects were observed. These results cast much doubt on the long-term effectiveness and on the practicality of certain recommendations aimed at lowering blood cholesterol levels through modifications in the type of dietary fat now consumed by the public at large.

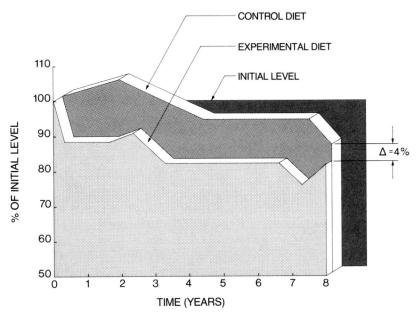

Fig. 50.—Serum cholesterol levels in men on a blood-cholesterol lowering diet as compared to controls.

(Adapted from Dayton et al[16].)

This study was carried out in Los Angeles with the aim of showing that changes in dietary habits could result in a lowering of serum cholesterol levels and, hence, in reducing mortality in a given population. Serum cholesterol in subjects fed a low-cholesterol low-saturated fat and high PUFA diet remained at a lower level than in controls during the entire experimental period. On the average, serum cholesterol levels in the experimental subjects were 12 per cent lower than in controls. At the end of the experiment, however, that is after eight years, the difference between the two groups was only 4 per cent and not statistically significant. As for mortality, it was the same for both groups. On a long-term basis, the effect of major changes in the type of dietary fat on serum cholesterol would be insignificant and probably of no practical consequence.

---

faults in the experimental procedure, such as insufficient number of subjects, inadequate controls, insufficient data concerning the diet actually consumed and too many drop-outs[1,12,21,22].

The Los Angeles intervention[16], however, was carried out under the most satisfactory experimental conditions, according to all impartial reports. It is important, then, to observe that in this major intervention study there was no difference in mortality between the group fed the high PUFA diet and that fed the normal or control diet. The authors reported 133 deaths in the experimental group as opposed to 141 in the control group. This small difference between the two groups was not statistically significant, which means that it might have been due to chance alone.

Nevertheless, there were fewer relapses and less mortality from cardiovascular disease in the experimental subjects than in controls. Unfortunately the number of cancers and other diseases was appreciably higher in subjects consuming the high PUFA diet than in the control subjects and the number of deaths, in the end, was the same for both groups.

From the major primary interventions based on drastic changes in the fat composition of the diet, we must repeat once more that the lipid hypothesis was not supported by the experimental evidence. This is particularly true when total mortality is considered. As a result, those responsible for the elaboration of nutrition policies should remember that the lipid hypothesis is no more than a hypothesis and that its validity remains to be proved.

It should also be noted that a high PUFA diet*, in addition to not reducing mortality, does entail the risk of a sharp rise in blood cholesterol following the return to a normal diet. The Los Angeles study enables us to evaluate this risk. At the end of this study, the individuals consuming the high PUFA diet were allowed to return to the normal diet consumed by controls. Blood cholesterol rose abruptly by approximately 20 per cent and remained high until the end of the study, eight months later (Fig. 51). During that time, blood cholesterol in the control subjects remained unchanged and at a level consistently lower than in the experimental subjects who had consumed the high PUFA diet.

The change from a hypocholesterolemic to a normal diet, after a long period, may thus provoke a sudden rise of blood cholesterol. This rise may even exceed significantly the level which would have been observed had the regular diet been maintained. Without attempting to draw final conclusions from such a study, it would seem that a diet poor in saturated fats, high in polyunsaturated fatty acids and low in cholesterol, might cause yet unidentified disorders in the metabolism of cholesterol which are still unpredictable. It is possible that a high-PUFA low-cholesterol diet might trigger adaptation mechanisms which result in a marked elevation in blood cholesterol as soon as the diet is abandoned. It is well known that adhering to a hypocholesterolemic diet is extremely difficult in everyday life. The eventual return to a normal diet is almost unavoidable. In view of this, one may wonder whether recommending a high-PUFA high-P/S ratio diet to the general public might not result in the long run in a rise in blood cholesterol rather than in a reduction.

---

* A high PUFA diet is always rich in linoleic acid (C18:2ω6) and poor in fats of animal origin.

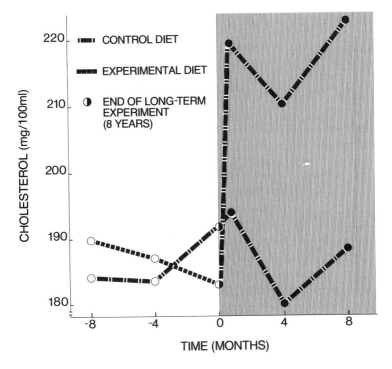

Fig. 51—Rise in blood cholesterol following a sudden change from a hypocholesterolemic to a normal diet.

(Taken from Dayton et al[16].)

At the end of the Los Angeles study, the experimental subjects consuming the high-PUFA low-cholesterol diet were allowed to return to the normal diet consumed by the control subjects. Blood cholesterol rose abruptly by approximately 20 per cent and remained high until the end of the study, eight months later. A sudden change from a high-PUFA low-cholesterol diet to a more normal one seems to cause some disorders in the metabolism of cholesterol. These disorders would appear to trigger certain adaptation mechanisms which result in a sudden and lasting elevation in blood cholesterol when the diet is abandoned.

Use of a hypocholesterolemic drug

The results of the primary intervention studies based on modifications of the diet did not support the validity of the lipid hypothesis. In view of this failure attention was directed towards specific hypocholesterolemic drugs to investigate the assumed beneficial effect of a lowering of serum cholesterol on mortality. Clofibrate is a drug that can reduce blood cholesterol in treated subjects.

A large-scale study[20] was carried out in three European cities: Edinburgh, Budapest and Prague, under the sponsorship of the World Health Organization. This study was designed to meet the requirements of biostatisticians. At least 10,627 men aged 30–59 completed the experiment, which lasted five years. It should be noted that the subjects were selected from a group of men whose blood cholesterol was, on average, 250 ml per 100 ml of serum which corresponds to the highest tertile in the general public. The results were published in 1978[20].

As indicated in Table 17, clofibrate caused a reduction in blood cholesterol of approximately 9 per cent compared to the untreated control subjects. Such a small drop was disappointing since a reduction of about 15 per cent had been anticipated. More disappointing yet was the fact that mortality from heart attacks was similar in both the treated and untreated subjects: 1.3 per 1,000 persons per year for the treated subjects as compared to 1.2 for the untreated control subjects. In fact, mortality was slightly higher in the treated subjects, but the slight difference between the two groups was not statistically significant.

Mortality from all causes, however, was significantly higher in the subjects treated with clofibrate than in subjects receiving the placebo: 4.9 per 1,000 persons per year in the treated subjects compared to 3.8 for the untreated control subjects. A higher incidence of cancers in the treated subjects explained in part the difference observed in total mortality. In addition to a higher incidence of cancer, there was a higher incidence of gallstones in the treated subjects when compared to controls: 59 cases in the subjects treated with clofibrate as compared with 24 in subjects receiving the placebo.

Nevertheless, a close examination of the results revealed that the incidence of non-fatal myocardial infarction was somewhat lower in men receiving clofibrate than in control subjects. In spite of the slight beneficial effect of clofibrate on total mortality, the higher incidence of cancers and gallstones in the treated subjects led the authors to conclude that this drug should not be recommended for general use by the public[20].

Those who believed in the lipid hypothesis saw some hope in this study, because non-fatal myocardial infarction was less frequent in subjects whose serum cholesterol was reduced by clofibrate. Unfortunately, this apparently beneficial effect did not reduce mortality from ischemic heart disease.

In conclusion, the results of the major primary interventions, based on drastic modifications in the lipid composition of the diet or on the use of a hypocholesterolemic drug, strongly suggest that it may be impossible to reduce mortality by means of diets high in polyunsaturated fatty acids and low in fats of animal origin.

SECONDARY PREVENTION INTERVENTION STUDIES

The secondary intervention studies, like the primary studies, arose from the lipid hypothesis, but in this case the experimental procedure was aimed at reducing blood cholesterol in persons who had previously had heart attacks. According to the hypothesis, a lowering of blood cholesterol should cause a reduction in the incidence of relapses and in mortality. As in the primary studies, drastic modifications of the lipid composition of the diet and use of hypocholesterolemic drugs were investigated.

Changes in the lipid composition of the diet

The secondary intervention studies based on modifications to the lipid composition of the diet were carried out during the 1960s and early 1970s. At that time the studies of Beveridge at Western University, Ontario, and of Keys at the University of Minnesota, to mention only two, suggested that atherosclerosis was caused by a high intake of saturated animal fats and cholesterol. It was expected that the substitution of animal fats in the diet by vegetable oils high in polyunsaturated fatty acids* would retard the development of atherosclerosis, prevent cardiovascular disease and reduce mortality.

The major intervention studies (Table 18) based on such changes in the diet were carried out in London, Oslo, New Jersey and Sydney. In the first studies[23,24], substantial amounts of corn oil and soybean oil were added to the diet of men less than 70 years of age. These studies lasted from two to seven years. In addition to being requested to ingest large amounts of vegetable oil, the patients were asked to reduce their intake of eggs, milk, butter and meat.

In the Oslo experiment[25], the diet was low in saturated fatty acids and in cholesterol and high in polyunsaturated fatty acids*. The P/S ratio of the fat portion of the high-PUFA diet was 2.4 as compared with a ratio varying from 0.2 to 0.4 for the control diet. The P/S ratio of the control diet was considered normal for the type of diet generally consumed in Norway.

The New Jersey experiment[26] also evaluated diets high in PUFA and low in saturated fatty acids and cholesterol. Unfortunately, in this study, the control group belonged to a population different from that of the two experimental groups.

A direct comparison between the treated and the experimental groups was not possible from the statistical point of view. Nevertheless, in the course of the study, subjects were divided into comparable groups each receiving a different type of diet. The experimental diet was high in PUFA,

---

* *Mainly linoleic acid (C18:2ω6).*

low in saturated fatty acids, and its P/S ratio was 2.6 as compared to 0.34 for the control diet. The subjects consuming these two diets could be used for reliable comparisons.

The fifth major intervention study was carried out in Sydney, Australia[27]. It lasted 2–7 years and included 458 men aged 30–59 who had experienced clinical coronary disease at entry. The most modern methods in biostatistics were used to analyze the data.

The results of these major intervention studies are summarized in Table 18. It is to be noted that the serum cholesterol level was lowered by 5–17 per cent in subjects consuming the high PUFA diet as compared to controls; the weigh.ed average was less than 10 per cent. This value was similar to that observed in primary interventions.

In the London experiment[23], the subjects consumed 64 g of corn oil daily. This intake of vegetable oil, high in linoleic acid, lowered blood cholesterol but had no effect on the incidence of relapses, nor on mortality. On the contrary, mortality was higher in patients treated with corn oil than in those maintaining their regular food habits. The authors concluded that corn oil not only had no beneficial effect on the incidence of ischemic heart disease, but could even be harmful[23]. Thus, a high intake of corn oil which is naturally rich in linoleic acid, was not recommended for the prevention of ischemic heart disease.

In the second London study[24], soybean oil instead of corn oil was used. The patients ingested 80 g of soybean oil daily for periods of 2–7 years. As in the first study, the intake of high PUFA diet* with a P/S ratio of 2.0 was strongly recommended to patients under treatment. The report of an independent dietitian indicated that the patients on the experimental diet consumed about 108 mg of cholesterol per 1,000 kcal per day, as compared with nearly 260 mg for patients who maintained their regular diet. The P/S ratio of the fat portion of the experimental diet was really 2.0, as anticipated, by comparison to 0.17 for the controls who maintained their regular food habits. At the end of the study 25 deaths due to major relapses of ischemic heart disease had been noted in each of the two groups. Therefore, no beneficial effect could be attributed to the use of soybean oil, although serum cholesterol was significantly lowered in patients consuming the high PUFA diet when compared to controls. The authors concluded: "There is no evidence from the London study that the relapse-rate in myocardial infarction is materially affected by the unsaturated fat content of the diet used"[23].

The Oslo intervention[25] was carried out under more rigidly controlled conditions than the London studies. Consequently, the conclusions drawn from it should be even more reliable. Here again the high PUFA low

---

* A high PUFA diet is necessarily rich in linoleic acid (C18:2ω6) and low in fat of animal origin.

cholesterol diet (Table 18) induced a statistically significant drop in serum cholesterol, a drop which was maintained throughout the experiment. In spite of this lowering effect on blood cholesterol, the number of sudden deaths at the end of the experiment was exactly the same in both groups. For certain types of cardiac attack, however, the number of relapses was lower in the patients consuming the hypocholesterolemic diet than in the control patients. For all practical purposes, however, the act of consuming a diet which is insipid, dull, repetitive and unattractive to most people, as all diets high in polyunsaturated fat are, was not compensated by a reduction in mortality.

The results of the New Jersey study[26] were similarly disappointing. The authors concluded that the degree of unsaturation of the dietary fat had no influence on mortality from cardiovascular disease.

Lastly, the Sydney study[27] confirmed the observations made in all other secondary intervention studies to the effect that polyunsaturated fat and the P/S ratio were ineffective in reducing mortality from coronary heart disease. As a matter of fact, in this study, survival was significantly better in the group of patients consuming the saturated fat diet than in the group consuming the high-PUFA high-P/S-ratio diet.

To summarize, the five major intervention studies, based on drastic modifications of the fat composition of the diet in order to reduce blood cholesterol, give little support to the lipid hypothesis. On the contrary, they tend to demonstrate that the intake of polyunsaturated fat high in linoleic acid, accompanied by a decrease in the intake of cholesterol and saturated fat, is ineffective in a secondary prevention program for coronary heart disease.

Use of hypocholesterolemic drugs

The proponents of the lipid hypothesis had hoped that modifications of the fat composition of the diet would be helpful in the prevention of ischemic heart disease. Many nutritionists also had hoped that the intervention studies mentioned above would give scientific evidence as to the effect that the type of fat used in the diet would have in a prevention program for ischemic heart disease. Unfortunately, the major intervention studies gave little support to the lipid hypothesis and left the nutritionists without conclusive evidence one way or the other. That is why hypocholesterolemic drugs attracted much attention. The drugs which have been investigated are: oestrogen, dextrothyroxine, clofibrate and niacin. During the 1970s at least seven important reports were published giving the results of major secondary intervention studies based on the use of these drugs. Such studies were carried out in Great Britain and in the United States of America. They involved a large number of men and women aged 30–65. Each study lasted from two to six years.

TABLE 18

SUMMARY OF SECONDARY PREVENTION STUDIES BASED ON RADICAL CHANGES IN THE DIET

Source	Diet	CHOL[1]	P/S ratio	Period (years)	Number of men (age)	Δ CHOL[2]	Influence on mortality from CVD[3]
London, 1965[23]	Corn oil (64 g/day)	?	?	2	80	−17	None; possible toxicity; undesirable side effects.
London, 1968[24]	Soybean oil (80 g/day)	108	2.0	2–7	393	−10	None; not recommended; undesirable side effects.
Oslo, 1966[25]	Low in SFA[4] High in PUFA[4] Low in CHOL[4]	110	2.4	5	412 (30–64)	−14	None; but reduced number of relapses for some cardiovascular troubles.
New Jersey, 1973[26]	Low in SFA High in PUFA Low in CHOL	130	2.6	10	100 (30–50)	−8	None; PUFA inefficient.[5]
Sydney, 1977[27]	Low in SFA High in PUFA Low in CHOL	*	1.7	2–7	458 (30–39)	−5	Number of deaths was slightly greater in the high PUFA group.

[1] Dietary intake of cholesterol as mg per 1,000 kcal per day
[2] Change in the concentration of serum cholesterol in percentage in comparison with the control subjects
[3] Cardiovascular disease

[4] SFA: saturated fatty acids
PUFA: polyunsaturated fatty acids, mainly linoleic acid ($C18:2\omega6$)
CHOL: dietary cholesterol (mg/1000 kcal)
[5] For sub-groups with adequate controls
* 300 mg or less per day

This table presents a summary of the five major secondary intervention studies which were carried out to investigate the influence of drastic changes in the fat composition of the diet on mortality due to ischemic heart disease. The changes in the diet consisted of a large increase in the intake of polyunsaturated fatty acids (mainly linoleic acid) and a large reduction in the intake of cholesterol and saturated fats. In all cases, the serum cholesterol level fell in the subjects on the experimental diets by comparison with the control subjects, but such drastic changes proved ineffective in reducing total mortality. The consumption of large amounts of polyunsaturated fat had to be abandoned in one experiment and was considered not acceptable in another. In one study survival was significantly better in the group of patients consuming the saturated fat diet than in those consuming the high PUFA diet. It was, therefore, impossible to show that changes in the kind of fat consumed could have any effect in the prevention of ischemic heart disease. It must be concluded that the lipid hypothesis has gained little support from these secondary intervention studies.

TABLE 19

SUMMARY OF SECONDARY INTERVENTION STUDIES BASED ON THE USE OF HYPOCHOLESTEROLEMIC DRUGS

Source	Drug	Number of subjects[1]	Duration (years)	Δ CHOL[2]	Year of report	Effect on mortality from CHD[3]
The Coronary Drug Project[28-31]	Oestrogen (5.0 mg/day)	3,907 ♂	2	—	1970	None. Discontinued. Undesirable side-effects.
	Oestrogen (2.5 mg/day)	3,890 ♂	5	—	1973	None. Discontinued. Undesirable side-effects. High incidence of gallstones.
	Dextro-thyroxine (6.0 g/day)	3,790 ♂	3	−10	1972	Higher mortality rate.
	Niacin (3 g/day)	3,908 ♂	5	−10	1975	None. Not recommended.
	Clofibrate (1.8 g/day)	3,892 ♂	5	−6	1975	None. Not recommended. High incidence of gallstones. Undesirable side-effects.
Scottish Society of Physicians[32]	Clofibrate (1.6 or 2.0 g/day)	717 ♂ + ♀	6	−10	1971	Variable with no relation to the blood lipid level.
Newcastle Upon Tyne[33]	Clofibrate (1.6–2.0 g/day)	497 ♂ + ♀	5	−9	1971	Variable with no relation to the blood lipid level.

[1] Including the control subjects
[2] Change in the concentration of serum cholesterol in percentage as compared to control subjects
[3] Coronary heart disease

This table presents a summary of the results obtained in the seven major secondary interventions where four hypocholesterolemic drugs were investigated. A small reduction in blood cholesterol was observed in all cases, less than 9 per cent on the average. The results of these studies showed no effect on mortality. The use of some of the drugs was abandoned; none was recommended. Lowering blood cholesterol by about 10 per cent was ineffective in preventing mortality from coronary heart disease. These major secondary intervention studies gave little support to the lipid hypothesis.

The first two studies evaluated the use of oestrogen[28-31]. After two years of experimentation, it was found that this drug had no influence on mortality in treated subjects as compared with control subjects (Table 19). This hormone had undesirable side-effects in men. The doses were then reduced but the investigators came to the same conclusions after five years of experimentation: oestrogen had no effect on mortality and showed undesirable side-effects.

Dextrothyroxine[29] was used in the second study and was given as a dose of 6.0 g per day. After three years, the serum cholesterol levels in men receiving this drug were lowered by less than 9 per cent when compared with control subjects (Table 19), but mortality was higher in the treated men. For that reason the study was discontinued. ·

Niacin[31] is a vitamin with hypocholesterolemic properties. Its usefulness as a blood cholesterol lowering agent was investigated in a five-year intervention study in 3,908 men. As predicted, it induced a drop in serum cholesterol of 10 per cent as compared to controls (Table 19). Lowering blood cholesterol, however, had no effect on mortality. Treatment with niacin, therefore, was not recommended as a secondary prevention method for coronary heart disease.

Clofibrate was unquestionably the drug that drew most attention[31-33]: it was investigated in several countries, both in men and in women. Following clofibrate treatment, serum cholesterol levels were lowered by about 9 per cent compared with control subjects receiving a placebo (Table 19). In Great Britain, the effect of clofibrate on total mortality was inconsistent and without any relationship to the blood lipid level. In the United States of America, the drug had no effect on mortality. Clofibrate was not recommended because of undesirable side-effects, especially a higher incidence of gallstones.

It can be concluded that the major secondary intervention studies based on the use of hypocholesterolemic drugs, like others based on changes in diet, have given little support to the lipid hypothesis. The drugs used were oestrogen, dextrothryroxine, niacin and clofibrate. These drugs lowered blood cholesterol by less than 9 per cent but this reduction of blood cholesterol did not lower mortality. In most cases these drugs induced such undesirable side-effects that they were not recommended for general use in secondary prevention programs for coronary heart disease.

SUMMARY

In summary, it can be said that the major intervention studies were disappointing to those who had placed much hope in lowering mortality from coronary heart disease by changing the fat composition of the diet. Drastic changes in the composition lowered the serum cholesterol level by less than 9 per cent and had no effect on total mortality. In some studies, a higher incidence of cancer was also observed in persons consuming the modified diets high in linoleic acid, the major polyunsaturated fatty acid in vegetable oils. The use of hypocholesterolemic drugs was as ineffective as the high-PUFA low-cholesterol diets both in lowering blood cholesterol and in reducing total mortality. The major intervention studies gave little support to the lipid hypothesis, according to which a lowering of blood cholesterol would lower mortality from coronary heart disease. In view of the results obtained in the major intervention studies the following conclusions would appear justified:

> *Increasing the consumption of fats rich in polyunsaturated fatty acids* and decreasing the intake of cholesterol and fats of animal origin is ineffective in prevention programs designed to reduce the incidence of coronary heart disease.*

REFERENCES

1. Borhani NO: Primary prevention of coronary heart disease: a critique. *Am J Cardiol*, 40:251–259, 1977
2. Keys A: Coronary heart disease in seven countries. American Heart Association, Monograph 29. *Circulation*, 41:suppl 1, 1970
3. Masironi R: Dietary factors and coronary heart disease. *Bull WHO*, 42:103–114, 1970.
4. Armstrong BK, Mann JI, Adelstein AM, Eskin F: Commodity consumption and ischemic heart disease mortality, with special reference to dietary practices. *J Chron Dis*, 28:455–469, 1975
5. Kannel WB: Some lessons in cardiovascular epidemiology from Framingham. *Am J Cardiol*, 37:269–282, 1976
6. Stamler J: Population studies. In Levy RI, Rifkind BM, Dennis BH, Ernst ND (eds) *Nutrition, Lipids, and Coronary Heart Disease. A Global View*, p 57. New York, Raven Press, 1979
7. Tyroler HA, Heyden S, Bartel A, Cassel J, Cornoni JC, Hames CG, Kleinbaum D: Blood pressure and cholesterol as coronary risk factors. *Arch Intern Med*, 128:907–914, 1971
8. Miller NE, Thelle DS, Førde OH, Mjøs OD: The Tromsø heart-study. High-density lipoprotein and coronary heart-disease: a prospective case-control study. *Lancet*, 1:965–970, 1977
9. Robertson TL, Kato H, Gordon T, Kagan A, Rhoads GG, Land CE, Worth RM, Belsky JL, Dock DS, Miyanishi M, Kawamoto S: Epidemiologic studies of coronary heart disease and stroke in Japanese men living in Japan, Hawaii and California. Coronary heart disease risk factors in Japan and Hawaii. *Am J Cardiol*, 39:244–249, 1977
10. McGee D, Gordon T: The Framingham Study—an epidemiological investigation of cardiovascular disease. Section 31. The results of the Framingham Study applied to four other U.S.-based epidemiologic studies of cardiovascular disease, U.S. Department of Health, Education, and Wel-

---

* *Mainly linoleic acid (C18 : 2ω6).*

fare. DHEW Publication No (NIH) 76-1083, Washington, DC, 1976

11. Tibblin G, Wilhelmsen L, Werkö L: Risk factors for myocardial infarction and death due to ischemic heart disease and other causes. *Am J Cardiol,* 35:514–522, 1975

12. Sherwin R: Controlled trials of the diet-heart hypothesis: some comments on the experimental unit. *Am J Epidemiol,* 108:92–99, 1978

13. Wright IS: Correct levels of serum cholesterol. Average *vs* normal *vs* optimal. *JAMA,* 236:261–262, 1976

14. Hulley SB, Rosenman RH, Bawol RD, Brand RJ: Epidemiology as a guide to clinical decisions. The association between triglyceride and coronary heart disease. *N Engl J Med,* 302:1383–1389, 1980

15. Turpeinen O, Karvonen MJ, Pekkarinen M, Miettinen M, Elosuo R, Paavilainen E: Dietary prevention of coronary heart disease: the finnish mental hospital study. *Int J Epidemiol,* 8:99–118, 1979

16. Dayton S, Pearce ML, Hashimoto S, Dixon WJ, Tomiyasu U: A controlled clinical trial of a diet high in unsaturated fat in preventing complications of atherosclerosis. *Circulation,* 40(suppl 2):1–63, 1969

17. Stamler J: Acute myocardial infarction—progress in primary prevention. *Br Heart J,* 33(suppl):145–164, 1971

18. Christakis G, Rinzler SH, Archer M, Krauss A: Effect of the anti-coronary club program on coronary heart disease risk-factor status. *JAMA,* 198:597–604, 1966

19. Miettinen M, Turpeinen O, Karvonen MJ, Elosuo R, Paavilainen E: Effect of cholesterol-lowering diet on mortality from coronary heart-disease and other causes. A twelve-year clinical trial in men and women. *Lancet,* 2:835–838, 1972

20. Oliver MF, Heady JA, Morris JN, Cooper J: A co-operative trial in the primary prevention of ischaemic heart disease using clofibrate. Report from the Committee of Principal Investigators. *Br Heart J,* 40:1069–1103, 1978

21. Halperin M, Cornfield J, Mitchell SC: Effect of diet on coronary-heart-disease mortality. *Lancet,* 2:438–439, 1973

22. Ahrens EH Jr: The management of hyperlipidemias: whether, rather than how. *Ann Intern Med,* 85:87–93, 1976

23. Rose GA, Thomson, WB, Williams RT: Corn oil in treatment of ischaemic heart disease. *Br Med J,* 1:1531–1533, 1965

24. Morris JN, Ball KP: Controlled trial of soya-bean oil in myocardial infarction. Report of a research committee to the medical research council. *Lancet,* 2:693–699, 1968

25. Leren P: The effect of plasma cholesterol lowering diet in male survivors of myocardial infarction. A controlled clinical trial. *Acta Med Scand,* 466(suppl):5–92, 1966

26. Bierenbaum ML, Fleischman AI, Raichelson, RI, Hayton T, Watson PB: Ten-year experience of modified-fat diets on younger men with coronary heart-disease. *Lancet,* 1:1404–1407, 1973

27. Woodhill JM, Palmer AJ, Leelarthalpin B, McGilchrist C, Blacket RB: Low fat, low cholesterol diet in secondary prevention of coronary heart disease. In Kritchevsky D, Paoletti R, Holmes WL (eds) *Drugs, Lipids and Atherosclerosis,* pp 317–330. New York, Plenum Press, 1977

28. Coronary Drug Project Research Group: The Coronary Drug Project. Initial findings leading to modifications of its research protocol. *JAMA,* 214:1303–1313, 1970

29. Coronary Drug Project Research Group: The Coronary Drug Project. Findings leading to further modifications of its protocol with respect to dextrothyroxine. *JAMA,* 220:996–1008, 1972

30. Coronary Drug Project Research Group: The Coronary Drug Project. Findings leading to discontinuation of the 2.5-mg/day estrogen group. *JAMA,* 226:652–657, 1973

31. Coronary Drug Project Research Group: Clofibrate and niacin in coronary heart disease. *JAMA*, 231:360–381, 1975

32. Oliver MF: Ischaemic heart disease: a secondary prevention trial using clofibrate. Report by a research committee of the Scottish Society of Physicians. *Br Med J*, 4:775–784, 1971

33. Anonyme: Trial of clofibrate in the treatment of ischaemic heart disease. Five-year study by a group of physicians of the Newcastle upon Tyne region. *Br Med J*, 4:767–775, 1971

8
General conclusions

As a nutritionist, the author would have liked to find irrefutable scientific evidence linking food habits to coronary heart disease. Such evidence would have provided hope for the prevention of ischemic heart disease even if major modification of the diet would have been necessary. Unfortunately, the large body of scientific data now available suggests that:

(1) *total blood cholesterol would seem to be only a poor indicator of the risk of developing coronary heart disease;*

(2) *dietary cholesterol, in general, has little influence on blood cholesterol;*

(3) *the major prevention intervention studies based on the use of hypocholesterolemic diets or drugs showed that the slight lowering of blood cholesterol levels induced by these diets and drugs had no effect on total mortality. In some instances, undesirable side-effects and a higher incidence of cancer were associated with the use of these diets and drugs. Thus, hypocholesterolemic diets high in polyunsaturated fatty acids (linoleic acid) and low in cholesterol and animal fat have little or no effect on coronary heart disease, and such diets are of little benefit in primary as well as in secondary prevention programs;*

(4) *diets high in polyunsaturated fatty acids (PUFA) do not seem to increase the serum levels of HDL—a class of lipoproteins becoming known as the "good" cholesterol; and*

(5) *the "lipid hypothesis," after repeated investigation in the past two decades, remains a hypothesis for which "completely satisfactory evidence has not yet been advanced either pro or con"[1].*

Some of these facts seem to have escaped the attention of many physicians, nutritionists, dietitians and other health professionals. In consequence the *lipid hypothesis* has been accepted by some as an indisputable truth and is inspiring nutrition and food policies. This hypothesis has led to hasty recommendations aimed at drastic changes in the food habits of people living in industrialized countries. The Dietary Goals put forward by Senator McGovern's Select Committee, addressed to the citizens of the United States of America, is an example of the advocation of such drastic changes. These "Dietary Goals" have already influenced nutrition and food policies in Canada as well as in other industrialized countries[2-6]. This influence is still persisting in spite of the obvious resistance and disapproval, if not strong opposition, expressed by many[7-9].

In some countries, in Canada, for example, the recommended changes in food habits are not aimed primarily at reducing the intake of cholesterol[10], but rather at increasing the consumption of polyunsaturated fatty acids, linoleic acid in particular. The scientific data, however, suggest that an increased consumption of polyunsaturated fats, at the expense of animal fats, would be of no apparent benefit in preventing cardiovascular disease. Many are convinced that it is too soon to make recommendations to the public in this matter[11-13].

The recommendations aimed at increasing the intake of polyunsaturated fatty acids in the form of linoleic acid imply, almost inevitably, an increased consumption of foods processed with partially hydrogenated vegetable oils. Partially hydrogenated oils in general contain positional and geometrical isomers of naturally occurring fatty acids. Vegetable oils so processed may contain large amounts of various *trans* fatty acids. These isomers of the fatty acids occurring naturally in the unprocessed oils are becoming ubiquitous in our foods. *Trans* fatty acids may soon represent 10 per cent of the total fat in the diet of a good part of the population. It would appear important, therefore, to ascertain more precisely the wholesomeness of these compounds. The *trans* dienes are of particular concern.

In Canada, as in most industrialized countries, cardiovascular disease remains the principal cause of death. Fortunately, in Canada[14] and in the United States[15,16] ischemic heart disease mortality is rapidly decreasing. There may be many reasons for this decline and several explanations have been proposed[16]. It would appear, however that changes in food habits can account for at most a very small part of the reduction. Many changes in life style have occurred in the past 20 years, and a greater awareness in the general public of risk factors other than diet is obvious.

We are convinced that certain trends of thought concerning lipids in human nutrition are based on fragmentary information and that important observations have been neglected or soon forgotten. When all the information is taken into account, it is difficult not to be in agreement with the views expressed recently by Ahrens[1,11], Borhani[17], Blackburn[18], Mann[19], Kummerow[20], Reiser[21,22], Olson[23], Harper[8,9], Sir John McMichael[24], Oster[12], the National Academy of Sciences of the United States[7], the

National Nutrition Consortium[13] and many other investigators who have not yet spoken publicly. All these professors, investigators and scientific institutions, representing thousands of physicians, nutritionists, dieticians, and many other professionals interested in public health, agree that it was and still is premature, if not dangerous, to recommend major changes in the nature of fats consumed in countries such as ours, where foods are varied and of high quality, and where the life expectancy is already near 70 years.

REFERENCES

1. Ahrens EH Jr: The management of hyperlipidemias: whether, rather than how. *Ann Intern Med*, 85:87–93, 1976
2. Mustard JF, Little JA, Horlick L, Davignon J, Spence MW, Christie K: Rapport du comité sur le régime alimentaire et les maladies cardio-vasculaires. *Santé et Bien-être social Canada*, December, 1976
3. Anonyme: Recommendations for prevention programs in relation to nutrition and cardiovascular disease. *Can Home Econ J*, April:105–109, 1978
4. Anonyme: Le beurre une étude internationale. *Bureau laitier du Canada*, December, 1980
5. Spence M, Davignon J, Holub B, Little JH, McDonald BE: Report of the *ad hoc* committee on the composition of special margarines. Ottawa, December 5–7, 1979. *Minister of Supply and Service, Canada*, 1980
6. Apfelbaum M, Bour H, Jaillard J, Le Quintrec Y, Lesieur B, Polonovski J: Les lipides dans l'équilibre alimentaire. *Société des Publications Essentielles*, 1978
7. National Academy of Sciences: Toward Healthful Diets. Food and Nutrition Board, Division of Biological Sciences, Assembly of Life Sciences, National Research Council. Washington DC, *National Academy of Sciences*, 1980
8. Harper AE: Dietary goals—a skeptical view. *Am J Clin Nutr*, 31:310–321, 1978
9. Harper AE: Bad advice to congress: a critique. *Nutr Today*, May–June:22–26, 1979
10. Health and Welfare Canada. Recommendations for prevention programs in relation to nutrition and cardiovascular disease. Recommendations of the Committee on Diet and Cardiovascular Disease, as amended and adopted by Department of National Health and Welfare, June, 1977
11. Ahrens EH: Dietary fats and coronary heart disease: unfinished business. *Lancet*, 2:1345–1348, 1979
12. Oster KA: Duplicity in a committee report on diet and coronary heart disease. *Am Heart J*, 99:409–412, 1980
13. National Nutrition Consortium: Guidelines for a national nutrition policy. *Nutr Rev*, 38:96–98, 1980
14. Anonyme: Cardiovascular-renal mortality 1950–1968. Statistics Canada, Health and Welfare Division, Vital Statistics Section. Catalogue 84–529 occasional, March, 1973
15. Stallones RA: The rise and fall of ischemic heart disease. *Scientific American*, 243:53–59, 1980
16. Stern MP: The recent decline in ischemic heart disease mortality. *Ann Intern Med*, 91:630–640, 1979
17. Borhani NO: Primary prevention of coronary heart disease: a critique. *Am J Cardiol*, 40:251–259, 1977
18. Blackburn H: Coronary disease prevention. Controversy and professional attitudes. *Adv Cardiol*, 20:10–26, 1977

19. Mann GV: Current concepts. Diet-heart: end of an era. *N Engl J Med*, 297:644–650, 1977

20. Kummerow FA: Nutrition imbalance and angiotoxins as dietary risk factors in coronary heart disease. *Am J Clin Nutr*, 32:58–83, 1979

21. Reiser R: Oversimplification of diet: coronary heart disease relationships and exaggerated diet recommendations. *Am J Clin Nutr*, 31:865–875, 1978

22. Reiser R: The three weak links in the diet-heart disease connection. *Nutr Today*, 14:22–28, 1979

23. Olson R: Is there an optimum diet for the prevention of coronary heart disease? In Levy RI, Rifkind BM, Dennis BH, Ernst ND (eds) *Nutrition, Lipids, and Coronary Heart Disease, A Global View*, pp 349–364, New York, Raven Press, 1979

24. McMichael J: Fats and atheroma: an inquest. *Br Med J*, 1:173–175, 1979

Index